Torey Hayden was born in 1951 and took degrees in biology, special education and child psychology. She worked as a teacher with severely emotionally disturbed children for several years before going on to a state mental institution as the master teacher on the children's unit for a year and teaching at the University of Minnesota. She has undertaken extensive research into child psychopathology and has lectured on the subject in the United States, London and Hamburg.

Torey Hayden was born in Montana, USA, but now lives in North Wales and writes full-time.

One Child won the St Christopher Catholic Award and was a Literary Guild Selection.

'An excellent book, gripping, without pretension, and well worth reading'
Literary Review

One Child

TOREY L. HAYDEN

SPHERE BOOKS LIMITED
30-32 Gray's Inn Road, London WC1X 8JL

First published in Great Britain by
Souvenir Press Ltd 1981
Copyright © 1980 by Torey L. Hayden
Published by Sphere Books Ltd 1982

The author gratefully acknowledges permission to
quote from *The Little Prince* by Antoine de
Sainte-Éxupéry, copyright 1943, 1971 by Harcourt
Brace Jovanovich, Inc

Printed and bound in Great Britain by
Wm. Collins Sons & Co. Ltd, Glasgow

To Sheila R., of course

I am asked repeatedly about
the poem on my office wall.
It seems only right that
they should know the child
who wrote it. And I
only hope I have been half as
good a writer.

Prologue

For the better part of my adult life I have been working with emotionally disturbed children. The autumn of my freshman year in college I took a volunteer position in a day program for disturbed and disadvantaged preschoolers. From that season I have remained captivated by the perplexing aspects of mental illness in childhood. Since that time I have acquired three degrees; devoted several years as a teacher's aide, a teacher, a university instructor and a psychiatric researcher; lived in five states; and worked in private day-care centers, public schools, locked psychiatric wards and state institutions, all the while pursuing the elusive answers to these children, the magic keys that will finally open them to my understanding. Yet, within me, I have long known there are no keys, and that for some children, even love will never be enough. But belief in the human soul escapes all reason and flies beyond the frail fingers of our knowledge.

I am often asked about my work. Perhaps the commonest question is Isn't it frustrating? Isn't it frustrating, the college student asks, to live day to day with violence, poverty, drug and alcohol addiction, sexual and physical abuse, neglect and apathy? Isn't it frustrating, the regular classroom teacher asks, to work so hard for so little in return? Isn't it frustrating, they all ask, to know your greatest success will probably never have more than an approximation of normalcy; to know that these very little children have been sentenced to live a life which, by our standards, will never be productive, contributing, or normal? Isn't it frustrating?

No. No, it isn't really. They are simply children, frustrating at times as all children are. But they are also gratifyingly compassionate and hauntingly perceptive. Madness alone seems to allow the whole truth to be spoken.

But these children are more. They are courageous. While we turn on the evening news to hear of new excitements and conquests on some distant front, we miss the very real dramas that play themselves out among us. This is unfortunate, because there is bravery here unsurpassed by any outside event. Some of these children live with such haunted nightmares in their heads that every move is fraught with unknown terror. Some live with such violence and perversity that it cannot be captured in words. Some live without the dignity accorded animals. Some live without love. Some live without hope. Yet they endure. And for the most part they accept, not knowing any other way.

This book tells of only one child. It was not written to evoke pity. Nor was it intended to bring praise on one teacher. Nor to depress those who have found peace in not knowing. Instead, it is an answer to the question of frustration in working with the mentally ill. It is a song to the human soul, because this little girl is like all my children. Like all of us. She is a survivor.

CHAPTER 1

I SHOULD HAVE KNOWN.

The article was a small one, just a few paragraphs stuck on page six under the comics. It told of a six-year-old girl who had abducted a neighborhood child. On that cold November evening, she had taken the three-year-old boy, tied him to a tree in a nearby woodlot and burned him. The boy was currently in a local hospital in critical condition. The girl had been taken into custody.

I read the article in the same casual manner that I read the rest of the newspaper and felt an offhand what-is-this-world-coming-to revulsion. Then later in the day it came back to me while I was washing the dishes. I wondered what the police had done with the girl. Could you put a six-year-old in jail? I had random Kafkaesque visions of the child knocking about in our old, drafty city jail. I thought about it only in a faceless, impersonal manner. But I should have known.

I should have known that no teacher would want a six-year-old with that background in his or her classroom. No parent would want a child like that attending school with his or her child. No one would want that kid loose.

I should have known she would end up in my program.

I taught what was affectionately referred to in our school district as the "garbage class." It was the last year before the effort to mainstream special children would begin; it was the last year to pigeonhole all the odd children into special classes. There were classes for the retarded, classes for the emotionally disturbed, classes for the physically handicapped, classes for the behaviorally disordered, classes for the learning disabled, and then there was my class. I had the eight who were left over, the eight who defied classification. I was the last stop before the institution. It was the class for young human refuse.

The spring before I had been teaching as a resource person, supplying help to emotionally disturbed and learning disabled children who attended regular classrooms part of the day. I had been in the district for some time in a variety of capacities; so I had not been surprised when Ed Somers, the Director of Special Education, had approached me in May and had asked if I would be interested in teaching the garbage class the next fall. He knew I had had experience with severely disturbed children and that I liked small children. And that I liked a challenge. He chuckled self-consciously after saying that, aware of how contrived the flattery sounded, but he was desperate enough to try it anyway.

I had said yes, but not without reservations. However, I longed for my own classroom again with my own set of kids. I also wanted to be free of an unintentionally oppressive principal. He was a good-hearted man, but we did not see things in the same way. He objected to my casual dress, to my disorderly classroom, and to my children addressing me by my first name. These were minor issues, but like all small things, they became the major sore spots. I knew that by doing Ed the favor of taking this class, allowances would be made for my jeans and my sloppiness and my familiarity with the kids. So I accepted the job, confident that I could overcome any of the obstacles it presented.

My confidence flagged considerably between the signing of the contract and the end of the first day of school. The first blow came when I learned I was to be placed back into the same school I had been in and under the same principal. Now not only did he have to worry about me but also about eight very peculiar children. Immediately we were all placed in a room in the annex which we shared with the gymnasium and nothing else. We were totally isolated from the rest of the school. My room would have been large enough if the children had been older and more self-contained. But for eight small children and two adults, plus ten desks, three tables, four bookcases and countless chairs that seemed to mate and multiply in the night, the room was hopelessly crowded. So out went the teacher's desk, two bookshelves, a file cabinet, all but nine little chairs and eventually all the student desks. Moreover, the room was long and narrow with only one window at the far end. It had originally been designed as a testing and counseling space, so it was wood-paneled and carpeted. I would have gladly traded all that grandeur for a room that did not need lights on all day or for a linoleum floor more impervious to spills and stains.

The state law required that I have a full-time aide because I was carrying the maximum load of severely disturbed children. I had been hoping for one of the two competent women I had worked with the year before, but no, I received a newly hired one. In our community, which had in close proximity a state hospital, a state prison and a huge migrant workers' camp, there was a staggering welfare list. Consequently, unskilled jobs were usually reserved for the unemployed listed with Social Services. Although I did not consider my aide position an unskilled one, Welfare did, and the first day of school I was confronted with a tall, gangly Mexican-American who spoke more Spanish than English. Anton was twenty-nine and had never graduated from high school. Well, no, he admitted, he had never worked with children. Well, no, he never especially wanted to. But you see, he explained, you had to take the job they gave you or you lost benefits. He dropped his gargantuan frame onto one of the kindergarten-sized chairs, mentioning that if this job worked out, it would be the first time he had ever stayed north all winter instead of following the other migrant workers back to California. So then we were two. Later, after the school year started, I acquired a fourteen-year-old junior high school student who devoted her two hours of study hall to coming over and working with my class each day. Thus armed, I met the children.

I had no unusual expectations for these eight. I had been in the business long enough to have lost my naiveté. Besides, I had learned long before that even when I was shocked or surprised, my best defense was to never show it. It was safer that way.

The first to arrive that morning in August had been Peter. Eight years old and a husky black with a scraggly Afro, Peter had a robust body that belied the deteriorating neurological condition that caused severe seizures and increasingly violent behavior. Peter burst into the room in anger, cursing and shouting. He hated school, he hated me, he hated this class and he wasn't going to stay in this shitty room and I couldn't make him.

Next was Tyler, who startled me by being a girl. She slunk in behind her mother, her dark curly head down. Tyler was also eight and had already tried to kill herself twice. The last time the drain cleaner she had drunk had eaten away part of her esophagus. Now her throat bore an artificial tube and numerous red-rimmed surgical scars in ghoulish testimony to her skill.

Max and Freddie were both hauled in screaming. Max, who was a big, strapping, blond six-year-old, carried the label of infantile autism. He cried and squawked and twirled around the room flapping his hands. His mother apologized because he always acted so unpredictably to change. She looked at me wearily and let the relief to be free of him for a few hours show too plainly in her eyes. Freddie was seven and weighed 94 pounds. The fat rolled over the edges of his clothing and squeezed out between the buttons on his shirt. Once allowed to flop on the floor, he ceased crying, ceased everything, in fact, to lie lifelessly in a heap. One report said that he, too, was autistic. One stated that he was profoundly retarded. One admitted not knowing.

I had known Sarah, age seven, for three years. I had worked with her when she was in preschool. A victim of physical and sexual abuse, Sarah was an angry, defiant child. She had been electively mute throughout the previous year when she had been in a special first grade class at another school. She had refused to talk to anyone except her mother and sister. We smiled upon seeing each other, both of us thankful for a familiar face.

A smartly dressed, middle-aged woman carried in a beautiful, doll-like child. The little girl looked like a picture from a children's fashion magazine, her soft blond hair carefully styled, her crisp dress spotless. Her name was Susannah Joy, she was six, and this was her first time in school. My heart winced. To be placed in my class upon entrance to school was not a hopeful sign. The doctors had told the parents that Susannah would never be normal; she was a childhood schizophrenic. She apparently hallucinated both visually and auditorily, and spent most of her days weeping and rocking her body back and forth. She rarely spoke and even when she did, seldom meaningfully. The mother's eyes implored me to perform the magic ritual necessary to turn her fairy child back to normal. My heart ached seeing those pleading eyes, because they signified nonacceptance. I knew the pain and agony that lay ahead for those parents as they learned that none of us would ever have the type of magic they needed for Susannah Joy.

Last to come were William and Guillermo. Both were nine. William was a lanky, pasty-faced boy haunted by fears of water and darkness and cars and vacuum cleaners and the dust under his bed. To protect himself, William engaged in elaborate rituals, compulsively touching himself or chanting little spells under his breath. Guillermo was one of the countless Mexican-American migrants who came to work in the fields each year. He was an angry boy but not uncontrollable. Unfortunately, he was also blind. At first I was stymied that he had been placed in my class, but was informed that the classes for the blind and partially sighted did not feel equipped to deal with his aggressive behaviors. Well, I thought, that made us even. I did not feel equipped to deal with his blindness.

So, then we were ten, and with Whitney, the junior high student, we were in all eleven. When first I surveyed this motley bunch of children and my equally motley staff, I felt a wave of despair. How would we ever be a class? How could I ever get them doing math or all the other miracles that needed accomplishing in nine months? Three were not toilet trained, two more had accidents. Three

13

could not talk, one wouldn't. Two would not shut up. One could not see. Certainly it was more of a challenge than I had bargained for.

But we managed. Anton learned to change diapers. Whitney learned to get urine out of the carpet. And I learned Braille. The principal, Mr. Collins, learned not to come over to the annex. Ed Somers learned to hide. And so we became a class.

By Christmas vacation we belonged to one another and I was beginning to look forward to each new day. Sarah had begun to talk regularly again; Max was learning his letters; Tyler was smiling occasionally; Peter didn't fly into rages quite so often; William could pass all the light switches in the hallway to the lunchroom and not say one charm to protect himself; Guillermo was begrudgingly learning Braille. And Susannah Joy and Freddie? Well, we were still trying with them.

I had read the newspaper article in late November and had forgotten it. But I shouldn't have. I should have known that sooner or later we would be twelve.

Ed Somers appeared in my room the day after school resumed following Christmas vacation. He came early, his kind face swathed in that apologetic expression that I was beginning to realize meant trouble for me. It was the expression attached to things like not getting a special tutor for Guillermo, or yet another hopeless report from the newest doctor Susannah's parents had found. Ed wanted things to be different; I believe he genuinely did, which made it impossible for me to be angry with him.

"There's going to be a new child in your class," he said, his face mirroring his hesitance to tell me.

I stared at him a long moment, not comprehending. I already had the state-allowed maximum and had never anticipated having another child. "I have eight now, Ed."

"I know, Torey. But this is a special case. We don't have any place to put her. Your class is the only option we have."

"But I've got eight kids already," I repeated dumbly. "That is all I can have."

Ed looked pained. He was a big bear of a man, tall and muscular like a football player but padded with the extra softness of middle age. His hair was nearly gone and what was left he had carefully combed across the shiny dome. But above all, Ed was gentle and I was amazed that he had ever made it to such a high position in education, a profession not known for its kind treatment of gentle people. But perhaps that was his secret, because I never failed to soften when he looked so hurt by what he was having to do to me.

"What's so special about this kid?" I asked tentatively.

"This is that girl who burned the little boy in November. They took her out of school and made arrangements to send her to the state hospital. But there hasn't been an opening in the children's unit yet. So the kid's been home a month and getting into all sorts of trouble. Now the social worker is beginning to ask why we aren't doing anything for her."

"Can't they put her on homebound?" I asked. A number of my children had been taught by homebound, a term referring to the practice of sending a teacher into the home to teach a child when for some reason he could not attend school. Often, severely disturbed children were handled in this manner until appropriate placement could be found.

Ed frowned at the floor. "No one is willing to work with her."

"The kid's six years old," I said in surprise. "They're scared of a six-year-old?"

He shrugged, his silence telling me more about this child than words could have.

"But I already have all the children I can handle."

"Choose a child to be transferred. We have to put this child in here, Torey. It will just be temporary. Until a place opens up at the state hospital. But we have to put her in here. This is the only place equipped to handle her. This is the only place she'll fit."

"You mean I'm the only one idiotic enough to take her."

"You can pick whom you want transferred."

"When is she coming?"

"The eighth."

By that point the children were beginning to arrive and I had to prepare for our first day back from vacation. Sensing my need to get to work, Ed nodded and left. He

15

knew that, if given time, I would do it. Ed knew that, for all my bravado, I was a pushover.

After telling Anton the news, I looked over the children. As we went through the day I kept asking myself who should go. Guillermo was the obvious choice, simply because I was least equipped to teach him. But what about Freddie or Susannah Joy? Neither was making progress of much note. Anyone could lug them around and change their pants. Or maybe Tyler. She wasn't so suicidal now; she hardly ever spoke of killing herself anymore; she no longer drew those black-crayoned pictures. A resource teacher could probably handle her. I looked at each one of them, wondering where they would go and how they would make it. And how our room would be without them. I knew in my heart none of them would survive the rigors of a less-sheltered class. None of them was ready. Nor was I ready to give them up, nor give up on them.

"Ed?" I clutched the receiver tightly because it kept slipping in my sweating hand. "I don't want to transfer any of my kids. We're doing so well together. I can't choose any one of them."

"Torey, I told you we have to put that girl in there. I'm really sorry. I hate to do it to you, but there isn't any other place."

I stared morosely at the bulletin board beside the phone with all its proclamations of events my children never could attend. I was feeling used. "Can I have nine?"

"Will you take nine?"

"It's against the law. Do I get another aide?"

"We'll see."

"Does that mean yes?"

"I hope so," Ed replied. "But we'll just have to see. Will you need another desk?"

"What I need is another teacher. Or another room."

"Will you settle for another desk?"

"No. I don't have any desks. There wasn't room for the first eight. So we just sit on the carpet or at the tables. No, I don't need another desk. Just send me the kid."

CHAPTER 2

SHE ARRIVED JANUARY EIGHTH. BETWEEN THE time I had agreed to accept her and the morning she arrived, I had heard nothing, received no files, learned no background. All I knew was what I had read in a two-paragraph article under the comics on page six a month and a half earlier. But I suppose it did not matter. Nothing could have prepared me adequately for what I got.

Ed Somers brought her, holding tightly on to her wrist and dragging her behind him. Mr. Collins also came out to the annex with Ed. "This is going to be your new teacher," Ed explained. "And this will be your new room."

We looked at one another. Her name was Sheila. She was six and a half, almost; a tiny little mite of a thing with matted hair, hostile eyes and a very bad smell. I was surprised she was so small. I had expected something bigger. The three-year-old must have been nearly as tall as she was. Clad in worn denim overalls and a well-faded boy's striped T-shirt, she looked like one of those kids in the Save the Children ads.

"Hi, my name's Torey," I said in my friendliest teacher's voice while reaching for her hand. But she did

17

not respond. I ended up taking the limp wrist from Ed. "This is Sarah. She's our welcome person. She'll show you around."

Sarah extended a hand but Sheila remained impassive, her eyes darting from face to face. "Come on, kid." Sarah grabbed her wrist.

"Her name is Sheila," I said. But Sheila bristled at these acts of familiarity and yanked her hand away, retreating backwards. She turned to run, but Mr. Collins was fortunately standing in the doorway and Sheila ran right into him. I captured one arm and dragged her back into the classroom.

"We'll leave you," Ed said, that apologetic look creeping across his face. "I left her cumulative folder in the office for you."

Anton slipped the bolt lock into place after closing the door behind Ed and Mr. Collins as they left. I dragged Sheila across the room to my chair where we always held morning discussion and set her on the floor in front of me. The other children cautiously gathered around us. Now we were twelve.

We always began each morning with "discussion." Ours was a school that enjoyed saying the pledge to the flag and singing patriotic songs before starting classes. I felt patriotism was not an appropriate topic for children who could not even communicate basic needs; however, the school board took a dim view of anyone who refused this display of nationalism. There were too many other issues I had to fight that were more important to me than the pledge of allegiance. So I compromised and created discussion. The children all came from such chaotic and disrupted homes that we needed something to reunite us each morning after being apart. And I had wanted something which would stimulate communication and develop verbal understanding. The first thing we did was the pledge, and I put it to good use by having one child lead it, which meant he had to learn it. Even this process was valuable because it presented words in an organized sense that implied meaning. Afterwards I started discussion with a "topic." Usually topic explored feelings, such as talking about things that made one happy; or topic was a roundtable for solving problems, such as what would one do if he saw someone else hurt himself. We went from there as a jumping-off point, making sure that everyone had a chance to participate. In the beginning I had brought all the topics in, but after the first month or two the children had their own suggestions and I had not started the discussion in ages.

After topic, I let each child have a few moments to tell what had happened to him since the release of school the previous day or Friday. These two aspects of morning discussion had gotten increasingly livelier, and even Susannah participated meaningfully on occasion. The kids all had a lot to say and I was hard put some days to terminate the activity. Afterwards, I outlined a schedule of the day and then we closed with a song. I had a repertoire of action songs that I could sing with more gusto than tune, usually pulling one of the kids through the actions puppetlike. The children loved that and we always ended laughing, even on those days when we had not come in merry.

So this morning I gathered the children around me. "Kids, this is Sheila, and she's going to join our class."

"How come?" Peter asked suspiciously. "You never told us we was getting a new girl."

"Yes, I did, Peter. Remember how we rehearsed last Friday things to show Sheila that we're glad she's with us? Remember what we did?"

"Well, I'm not glad she's with us," he replied. "I liked us just the way we was." He placed his hands over his ears to shut me out and began rocking.

"It'll take some getting used to, I imagine. But we will." I patted Sheila's shoulder and she pulled away. "Now, who's got a topic?"

Everyone sat around me on the floor. No one spoke.

"No one has a topic? Well then, I've got one: what do you suppose it feels like when you're new and don't know anyone, or maybe you want to be part of a group and no one wants you to? How's that feel inside?"

"Bad," Guillermo said. "That happened to me once and I felt bad."

"Can you tell us about it?" I asked.

Suddenly Peter leaped to his feet. "She stinks, teacher." He backed away from Sheila. "She stinks terrible and I don't want her sitting with us. She'll stink me up."

Sheila regarded him blackly but did not speak or move.

19

She had folded herself up into a little lump, her arms wrapped tightly around her knees.

Sarah stood up and moved around to where Peter had reseated himself. "She does stink, Torey. She smells like pee."

Good manners were certainly not our forte. I was not surprised by the lack of tact, but as always I was dismayed. Silencing their clear-eyed perceptions of the world was an impossibility. For every step forward I made in teaching good manners, I took two back and six to the side. "How do you suppose that feels, Peter, to have someone say you stink?"

"Well, she does stink terrible," Peter retorted.

"That's not what I asked. I asked how you'd feel if someone said that to you?"

"I wouldn't want to stink everybody out of the class, that's for sure."

"That's not what I asked."

"It'd hurt my feelings," Tyler volunteered, bouncing up on her knees. Any displays of anger or disagreement frightened Tyler tremendously and sent her into rounds of appeasement, acting overly mature for her eight years and motherly toward those who disagreed.

"How about you, Sarah?" I asked. "How would you feel?"

Sarah stared at her fingers, reluctant to look at me. "I wouldn't like it too good."

"No, I don't think any of us would. What might be a better way of handling the problem?"

"You could learn her in private that she stinked," William offered. "Then she wouldn't get embarrassed."

"You could learn her not to," Guillermo added.

"We could all plug our noses," Peter said. He wasn't quite willing to admit yet that he had been inappropriate in his remarks.

"That wouldn't help any, Peter," William said. "Then you couldn't breathe."

"You could too. You could breathe through your mouth."

I laughed. "Everybody, try Peter's suggestion. Peter, you too." All the children except Sheila plugged their noses and breathed through their mouths. I urged her to try too, but she steadfastly refused to unfold. In a few moments we were all laughing, even Freddie and Max, at the funny faces we made. All of us, except Sheila. I was beginning to fear that she saw this as a joke at her expense and I hastened to explain it wasn't. She ignored me, not even looking at me. This was the way we solved our problems, I told her.

"How's this make you feel?" I asked her at last. There was a long silence, pregnant with our waiting. The other children became impatient.

"Don't she talk?" Guillermo asked.

"I used to not talk either, remember that?" Sarah offered. "Back when I was mad, I used to never talk to nobody." She looked over at Sheila. "I used to never talk, Sheila. So I know how it feels."

"Well, I think we've put Sheila in the hot seat enough for now. Let's give her some time to get used to us, okay?"

We went on with the rest of morning discussion and finished with a rousing chorus of "You Are My Sunshine." Freddie clapped gleefully; Guillermo directed with his hands; Peter sang at the top of his lungs; and I manipulated Tyler like a rag doll. But Sheila sat, her face stormy, her little body a solid lump in the way of the dancers.

After discussion we dispersed for math activities. Anton began orienting the others while I showed Sheila around the room. Actually, I did not show her. I had to pick her up and carry her around from place to place because she would not move. I was thankful I was not teaching adolescents. Then when I got here where I wanted her, she refused to look, covering her face with her hands. But I hauled her around anyway, determined she become part of us. I showed her her cubby and her coat hook. I introduced her to Charles, the iguana, and Benny, the snake, and Onions, the rabbit who bit if you bothered him too much. I pointed out the plants we had started before Christmas that I had had to come in on vacation to water; and the stories we read before lunch every day; and the dishes we cooked with on Wednesday afternoons. I showed her our aquarium and our toys. I lifted her up to view the scene from our lone window. All this was accomplished by lugging her from place to place and chattering as if she were very interested in what I had to say.

21

But if she was, she did not let me know. She remained a dead weight in my arms, rigid and tense against my body. And she stank like an outhouse on a muggy July afternoon.

Finally I deposited Sheila on a chair at the table and got out a math paper. This evoked her first response. She grabbed the paper, wadded it up and threw it at me. I took another. She repeated the action. I took another. Again it was flung in my face. I knew I would run out of papers before she would run out of energy. So I took her on my lap, wrapping an arm around her wiry body so she could not get her hands free. I set another math paper down. It was simple addition; two plus one, one plus four, nothing fancy. I pulled a tray of blocks toward me with my free arm and spilled them on the table.

"Okay, now we do math," I stated. "First problem, two plus one." I showed her two blocks and added a third. "How much is that? Let's count them." She averted her head, straining her stiff body against me. "Can you count, Sheila?" No response. "Come on, I'll help. One, two, three. Two plus one is three." I picked up a pencil. "Here, we'll write it down."

Everything was a battle. I had to pry a hand free from her body, then uncurl her fingers, then place the pencil in it. Suddenly those tightly clenched fingers lost their strength and the pencil slid effortlessly out of them and onto the floor. In the moment I bent to pick up the pencil she had grabbed two blocks with her free hand and flung them across the room. I clutched at the hand, shoved the pencil back into it and tried to recurl her fingers around it and grip it with my own hand before she could let the pencil drop again. But she had me at a disadvantage; I was left-handed and forced to use that arm to subdue her in my lap. Having to use my right to perform all these dexterous movements, I was just not fast enough. Perhaps I would not have been even with my left. She was skilled at this little bit of guerilla warfare and the pencil fell again. After another struggle I gave up.

"Evidently you don't want to do math just yet. Okay, you may sit. I will say to you that everyone in here does his work and tries his best. But we're not going to fight about it. You want to sit, you sit." I lugged her over to the corner where I isolated the children when they became too over-stimulated and needed to regain control, or when they acted miserably, trying to command attention. I pulled the chair out and sat Sheila in it. Then I returned to the other children.

In a few moments I looked up. "Sheila, if you're ready to join us, you may come over."

She sat, her face to the wall and did not move. I let her sit. In another few minutes, I reissued the conditions. And again a little later. It was obvious that she was not going to do anything I wanted. I went over and pulled the chair away from the corner and into the room. Then I went back to the others. If she wanted to sit, she could. However, I was not going to let her isolate herself from us. If she sat, it would be right out in the middle of us.

Our morning routine went as usual. Sheila participated in nothing. Once ensconced upon that small wooden chair, she would not move, but instead drew in upon herself, folding knees up under her chin and wrapping her arms around them. She got off the chair one time to use the bathroom but returned to her seat to resume her contorted position. Even during recess she sat, only this time on the freezing cement. I had never seen such a motionless child. But her eyes followed me continuously everywhere I went. Brooding, angry, bitter eyes never left my face.

When lunch came, Anton helped the children prepare for their trek from the annex over to the cafeteria. Sheila had been lugged into line but I came and got her, taking her skinny wrist and pulling her out of the line. We waited until the others had gone. I looked down at her and she up at me. I thought that for a brief moment I saw an emotion other than hate flicker through those eyes, something other than anger. Fear?

"Come over here." I tugged her to the table and set her down in a chair opposite me. "You and I have something to get straight."

She glowered at me, her tiny shoulders humping up under the worn shirt.

"There aren't a lot of rules in this room. There are just two really, unless we need to make special rules for special times. But generally there are just two. One is that you can't hurt anybody in here. Not anybody else. And not yourself. The second is that you always try to do your best job. That's the rule I don't think you have straight yet."

She lowered her head slightly but kept her eyes on me. The legs came up and once again she began to fold in upon herself.

"You see, one of the things you have to do in here is talk. I know that's hard when you're not used to doing it. But in here you talk, that's part of your best job. The first time is always the hardest, and sometimes it kind of makes you cry. Well, that's okay to do in here. But you have to talk. And sooner or later you will. It'll be a lot better if you do it sooner." I looked at her, trying to match her unflinching stare. "Is that clear to you?"

Her face blackened with anger. I was fearful of what might happen if all that hate got loose, but I tried to squash the fear, not letting it show in my eyes. She was a good reader of eyes.

I had always felt strongly about setting expectations for my kids. Some of my colleagues had been skeptical of my directness with the children, pleading the frailty of their egos. I disagreed. While certainly all of them had sad, well-trampled little selves, none of them was frail. Much to the contrary. The fact that they had survived long enough to be where they were after what most of them had been through was testimony to their strength. However, all of them lived chaotic lives and brought chaos on others by the nature of their disturbance. I did not feel it was my right to add to the chaos by leaving them to guess what I expected of them. I found establishing a structure a useful and productive method with all the children because it erased the fuzziness of our relationship. Obviously, they had already shown they could not handle their own limits without help, or they never would have arrived in my class to begin with. As soon as the time came that they could, I began the process of transferring the power to them. But in the beginning I wanted there to be no doubt about what I expected from them.

So Sheila and I sat in icy silence while she digested this bit of information. I did not have the endurance to stare her down, nor did I feel the need to do so. After a few moments I rose from my chair and went to collect the math papers from the correction basket.

"You can't make me talk," she said.

I continued shuffling through the papers trying to find the marking pen. Three-fourths of being a good teacher is timing.

"I said you can't make me talk. There don't be no way you can do that."

I looked over at her.

"You can't make me."

"No, I can't." I smiled. "But you will. That's part of your job in here."

"I don't like you."

"You don't have to."

"I hate you."

I did not respond. That was one of those statements that I find is often best left unanswered. So I continued my search for the pen, wondering who had walked off with it this time.

"You can't make me do nothing in here. You can't make me talk."

"Maybe not." I dropped the papers back into the basket and came over to her. "Shall we go to lunch?" I extended a hand to her. Some of the anger had dissipated to be replaced by a less readable emotion. Then without further urging she got off the chair and came with me, careful not to touch me.

CHAPTER 3

AFTER ESCORTING SHEILA TO THE LUNCH-
room I retired to the office to have a look at her file. I
wanted to know what others had done with this perplexing
child. From watching her, it was apparent that she did not
suffer from the crippling, unexplainable disturbances such
as Max and Susannah displayed. Instead, she was in surprisingly good control of her behavior, more so than most
of the children coming into my class. Behind those hate-
filled eyes I saw a perceptive and most likely intelligent
little girl. She had to be in order to manipulate her world
with such conscious effort. But I wanted to know what
had been tried before.

The file was surprisingly thin for one that had worked
its way to me. Most of my children had thick, paper-
bloated folders, glutted with verbose opinions of dozens
of doctors and therapists and judges and social workers.
It was plain to me every time I read one of those files that
the people filling them never had to work with the child
day in and day out for hours at a time. The words on the
papers were erudite discourses, but they did not tell a
desperate teacher or frightened parent how to help. I
doubt anyone could write such words. In reality, each of
the children was so different and grew in such unpredict-

26

able ways that one day's experience was the only frame-work for planning the next. There were no textbooks or university courses specializing in Max or William or Peter.

But Sheila's file was thin, only a few bits of paper: a family history, test results and a standard data form from Special Services. I paged through the social worker's report of the family. Like so many others in my room, it was filled with lurid details that, despite my experience, my middle-class mind could not fully comprehend. Sheila lived alone with her father in a one-room shack in the migrant camp. The house had no heat, no plumbing, and no electricity. Her mother had abandoned Sheila two years earlier but had taken a younger son. She now lived in California, the form stated, although no one actually knew her whereabouts. The mother had been only four-teen when Sheila was born, two months after a forced wedding, while her father was thirty. I shook my head in grim amazement. The mother would only be twenty years old now, barely more than a child herself.

The father had spent most of Sheila's early years in prison on assault-and-battery charges. Since his re-lease two-and-a-half years before, he had also had stays at the state hospital for alcoholism and drug dependency. Sheila had been shifted around among relatives and friends of the family, mostly on the mother's side, before finally being abandoned on a roadside, where she was found clinging to a chain-link fence that separated the freeway lanes. Taken to the juvenile center, Sheila, then four, was discovered to have numerous abrasions and healed multiple fractures, all the results of abuse. She was released to her father's custody and a child-protection worker was assigned to the case.

A court statement appended to the file said that the judge felt it was best to leave the child in her natural home. A county-appointed physician had scrawled across the bottom that her small size probably resulted from malnutrition, but otherwise she was a healthy Caucasian female with well-healed scars and fractures. Loose behind these two assessments was a memo from the county's con-sulting psychiatrist with the single statement: Chronic Maladjustment to Childhood. I smiled at it in spite of myself; what an astute conclusion this man had drawn. How helpful to us all. The only normal reaction to

27

a childhood like Sheila's would be chronic maladjustment. If one did adjust to such pornography of life, it would surely be a testimony to one's insanity.

The test results were even more obscure. Beside each title on the battery, written in tight, frustrated printing: Refused. The bottom summary simply stated she was untestable and underlined the fact twice.

The Special Services questionnaire contained only demographics. The father had filled out the form and he had been in prison all those crucial years. She had been born with no apparent complications in a local hospital. Nothing was known of her early developmental history. She had attended three schools in her short educational history, not including the one she was in now. All the moves had resulted from her uncontrollable behavior. At home she was reported to eat and sleep within the normal limits. But she wet the bed every night and she sucked her thumb. She had no friends among the migrant workers' children at the camp; nor did she appear to have any solid relationships with adults. The father wrote that she was a loner, hostile and unfriendly even to him. She spoke erratically at home, usually only when she was angry. She never cried. I stopped and reread that statement. She never cried? I could not conceive of a six-year-old who did not cry. He must have meant she seldom cried. That must have been a mistake.

I continued reading. Her father saw her as a wayward child and disciplined her frequently, mostly by spanking or taking away privileges. I wondered what sort of privileges there were in her life to be taken away. In addition to the burning incident, she had been reprimanded for setting fires in the migrant camp and for smearing feces in the restroom of a bus station. By six-and-a-half, Sheila had encountered the police three times.

I stared at the file and its bits of random information. She was not going to be an easy child to love, because she worked at being unlovable. Nor was she going to be an easy child to teach. But she was not unreachable. Despite her exterior, Sheila was indeed probably more reachable than Susannah Joy or Freddie, because there was no indication that her functioning was garbled with retardation, or neurological impairments or other mysteries of the brain. From what I could glean, Sheila was a normally

28

functioning child in that respect. Which made the battle ahead for me even harder because I knew it rested solely with us on the outside. We had no cute phrases, no curtains like autism or brain damage to hide behind when we failed with the Sheilas. We had only ourselves. Deep down behind those hostile eyes was a very little girl who had already learned that life really isn't much fun for anybody; and the best way to avoid further rejection was to make herself as objectionable as possible. Then it would never come as a surprise to find herself unloved. Only a simple fact.

Anton came in while I was paging through the file. He pulled up a chair beside me and took the forms as I finished them. Despite our clumsy beginning, Anton and I had become a fully functioning team. He was an adroit worker with these children. Having spent all his life prior to this year in the fields, and still living in the migrant camp in a small hut with his wife and two sons, Anton knew much more intimately than I the world my kids came from. I had the training and the experience and the knowledge, but Anton had the instinct and the wisdom. Certain aspects of their lives I never would understand because in my existence warm houses and freedom from violence and hunger and cockroaches was my due. I had never had reason to expect otherwise. Now as an adult, I had learned that others lived differently and that this different way of life, to them, was also normal. I could accept the fact, but I could not understand it. I do not believe that anyone for whom it is not a living reality can; anyone claiming that extra measure of understanding either lies to himself or is a deluded braggart. But Anton compensated for my lack and together we had managed to build a supportive relationship. He had come to know without being told when and how and whom to help. An additional benefit was that Anton spoke Spanish, which I did not. Thus, he saved me innumerable times when Guillermo went beyond his limit of English. Now Anton sat beside me, quietly reading Sheila's folder.

"How did she do at lunch?"

He nodded without looking up from the papers. "Okay. She eats like she never sees food. But she probably doesn't. And, oh, so bad on the manners. But she sat with the children and did not fuss."

29

"Do you know her father out at the camp?"

"No. That's the other side of the camp, where the whites live. The junkies are all over there. We never go over."

Whitney came in and leaned over the counter. She was a pretty girl in a nondescript way: tall, slender, with hazel eyes and long, straight, dishwater-blond hair. Although Whitney was an honors student at her junior high and came from one of the community's most prominent families, she was a painfully shy girl. When she had come in the fall she had carried out all her tasks in great silence, never looking me in the eye, always smiling nervously, even when things were going wrong. The only time she did talk was to criticize her work, to put herself down or to apologize for doing everything wrong. Unfortunately, in the beginning that seemed all too true. Whitney made every mistake in the book. She dropped half a gallon of freshly mixed green tempera paint on the gym floor. She forgot Freddie in the men's room at the fairgrounds. She left the door to our room ajar one afternoon after school and Benny, the class boa constrictor, escaped and went to visit Mrs. Anderson, the first grade teacher. For me, Whitney was like having another child. If I had not been so desperate in those early months for a third set of hands to help, I might not have had the patience for her. Those first weeks I was always reexplaining, always cleaning something up, always saying, "Don't worry about it," when I did not mean it. Whitney was always crying.

But like Anton, Whitney had been worth the trouble, because she cared so much about the kids. Whitney was hopelessly devoted to us. I knew she skipped classes occasionally to stay longer with us, and she often came over on her lunch hour or after school to help me. From home she brought her own outgrown toys to give the children. She came with ideas for me that she had found in teaching magazines she read in her spare time. And always that hungry, pleading look to be appreciated. Whitney very seldom talked about the rest of her life outside my classroom. Yet, despite her affluence and the prominent name of her family, Whitney, I suspected, was no better off in some ways than the kids in the class. So I remained tolerant of her clumsiness and ineptitude and tried to make her feel a valued part of our team. Because she was.

"Did you get your new girl?" Whitney asked, stretching over the counter and causing her hair to tumble onto the papers I was reading.

"Yes, we did," I said and mentioned briefly what had transpired during the morning. That was when I heard the screaming.

I knew it was one of my children. None of the regular kids seemed to have that high vibrant note of desperation in their voices when they yelled. I looked at Anton, asking him wordlessly what was going on. Whitney went to look out the door of the office.

Tyler came careening in, wailing. She motioned out the door but her explanation was strangled in her sobs. Then she turned and ran.

All three of us sprinted after her toward the door that led to the annex. Normally over the lunch hour, lunch aides were in charge of the children. In the cold months, the kids all played inside in their rooms and the aides patrolled up and down the halls keeping order. I kept telling them that my children could not be left unattended at any time, but the aides hated supervising my room and avoided it by congregating outside the annex door and keeping an ear cocked for disaster. My children had the latest lunch hour, which meant the aides only had about twenty minutes of actual supervision. But they still protested and still refused to stay in the room with the kids. I usually ignored the aides, because I had worked hard to instill in my kids the independence to function without my physical presence. Lunch hour was a daily test of this skill. Moreover, both Anton and I desperately needed that half-hour break. Still things occasionally got out of hand.

Tyler was sobbing something out to us as we ran, something about eyes and the new girl. I came storming into a room in chaos.

Sheila stood defiantly on a chair by the aquarium. She had apparently caught the goldfish one by one and poked their eyes out with a pencil. Seven or eight of the fish lay flopping desperately on the floor around the chair, their eyes destroyed. Sheila clutched one tightly in her right fist and stood poised threateningly with the pencil in the other. A lunch aide was near her, dancing nervously about, but too frightened to attempt disarming Sheila.

31

Sarah was wailing, Max was flying about the room flapping his arms wildly and screeching.

"Drop that!" I shouted in my most authoritative voice. Sheila glared at me and shook the pencil meaningfully. I had no doubt she would attack if at all provoked. Her eyes had the glazed wildness of a threatened animal. The fish flopped hopelessly about, leaving little bloody spots on the floor where their empty eye sockets hit. Max crunched through one on his flight around the room.

Suddenly a high-pierced shriek knifed the air. Behind us Susannah had entered the room. She has a psychotic fear of blood, of any red liquid, and would go into a frenzy of crazed screaming while darting senselessly about when she thought she saw blood or even hallucinated it. Now, seeing the fish, she bolted off across the room. Anton moved after her and I took that moment of surprise to disarm Sheila who was not so off-guard as I had suspected. She slammed the pencil into my arm with such vehemence that for a moment it stuck, waving uncertainly before falling to the ground. My mind was filled with too much confusion to feel any real pain. Freddie had joined Max in circling the room. Tyler was wailing; Guillermo hid under the table; William stood in one corner and cried. Whitney was off trying to capture Max and Freddie as they reeled around the perimeter of the room screaming. The decibel level was unbearable.

"Torey!" came William's cry. "Peter's having a seizure!" I turned to see Peter collapse to the floor. Passing Sheila to Whitney, I ran for Peter to remove the chairs among which he had fallen.

Sheila gave Whitney an audible crack in the shins and won her freedom. Within seconds she was out the door. I fell onto the floor beside Peter, still writhing in his seizure, and felt the pressure of what was happening lie upon me. It had all happened within minutes. Everyone had lost the tenuous control we fought so hard to keep. All the children except Peter were crying. Sarah, Tyler and William wailed on the sidelines, their bodies huddled together against catastrophe. Guillermo sobbed from his retreat under the table. He kept his hands protectively over his head and pleaded in Spanish for his mother. Susannah struggled frantically in Anton's arms. Max and Freddie still flew deliriously around the room, colliding with furniture and other children only to rise and resume their flight. Peter lay incoherent in my arms. I looked around. Whitney had disappeared after Sheila. The lunch aide had left long ago. We were in shambles. After months and months of careful effort, everything had fallen around our ears.

Mr. Collins and the school secretary appeared in the doorway. Normally I would have been horrified to have him see my classroom in such distress. But things had gotten completely out of control and I needed help. I had to admit that. After all the years he and I had worked together, I had managed my crazy children and we had never had a major slip. But now I had failed. Just like he always predicted. My crazies had gotten loose at last. I knew he must be thanking God he had put us in the annex where no one could see.

The secretary took Peter to the nurse's office to be sent home because he always needed to sleep after a major seizure. Mr. Collins helped me round up Freddie and Max and get them to sit in chairs. I dragged poor Guillermo out from under the table and hugged him. What this must have sounded like to him, who could not see . . . Anton was still trying to soothe Susannah Joy. Once we seemed to recapture some semblance of control, Tyler and Sarah were willing to sit down in the discussion corner and comfort each other. But William remained glued to the spot, quaking and sobbing. Mr. Collins made an effort to calm him, but he could not bring himself close enough to hug the child. We kept crunching and sliding on the dead goldfish, grinding gold scales into the carpet, the sound our shoes made stepping on them a muffled squeak. At last I had all the kids herded together and the crying had diminished. Whitney and Sheila were still gone but I couldn't let myself think of that at that particular moment.

Mr. Collins had the decency not to ask what had happened. He had simply done as I asked, his face unreadable. When I got all the children settled down, I thanked him at the door for his help and asked if he could send me Mary, one of the regular school aides, who had been such a competent helper of mine the year before. I still had one on the loose, I explained, and the afternoon would be difficult. With one extra adult, I could get around to more of the children individually and try to set things straight.

When Mary arrived, the kids helped her choose a story they liked and I went in search of Sheila. Evidently when she had bolted, she was confused by the maze of doors and hallways connecting us to the main building. Whitney had been able to secure the outside doors before Sheila found them and she had been trapped into going into the gym, more by accident than design. Whitney stood in the doorway of the huge cavernous room and Sheila was on the far side.

Tears streamed over Whitney's cheeks as she held her post. My heart ached when I saw her. This was too much to expect of a fourteen-year-old. I should never have put her in this spot. Yet, my string of miracles had run out. Two adults alone could not manage that many disturbed children. I had been surviving on good luck, and now it had finally expired.

I entered the gym, gave Whitney a pat on the shoulder, and approached Sheila. She clearly had no intention of being caught. Her eyes were wild, her face flushed with terror. Each time I moved closer, she tore off in another direction. I spoke softly, my tone gentle and coaxing. But it quivered with my own frenzy. Slowly I edged closer. It did not matter. She could elude me forever in the huge gymnasium.

Pausing, I looked around, my mind racing for ideas. I had to catch her. Her eyes mirrored her uncontrolled panic. She had gone beyond the limits she could comprehend in the situation and was reacting from animal instinct alone now. At this point she was far more dangerous to herself and to others than back in the classroom with the fish.

I could not think what to do. My head pulsed. My arm throbbed where the pencil had sunk in. Blood had soaked through my shirt sleeve. If a number of us approached her, that would undoubtedly terrify her even more. If I boxed her in, that too would heighten her irrationality. She had to relax and regain some control of herself. She was too dangerous this way. Despite her size and her age, I had the experience to know that in this condition she posed a very real threat, if not to me, then to herself.

I went back to Whitney and told her to return to the classroom and tell Anton to manage as best he could with Mary. Then I closed the door to the gym. I pulled closed the heavy divider that separated the room into two parts, because I remembered it having a door in it that locked. I could not afford to let Sheila escape again. Then, together in the far half of the gym, I came as close to her as I dared and sat down.

We regarded each other. Frantic terror gleamed in her eyes. I could see her trembling.

"I'm not going to hurt you, Sheila. I'm not going to hurt you. I'm just going to wait until you're not so scared anymore and then we'll go back to class. I'm not angry. And I'm not going to hurt you."

Minutes passed. I scooted forward on my seat. She stared at me. The tremors had taken over her entire body and I could see her scrawny shoulders shake. But she did not budge.

I had been angry with her. God Almighty, I had been angry. Seeing our beloved fish on the floor, their eyes gouged out, I had been livid. I had an intolerance of cruelty to animals. But now the anger had faded and as I watched her, I was awash with pity. She was being so brave. Frightened and tired and uncomfortable, she refused to give in. Her world had been a very untrustworthy one and she was confronting it in the only way she knew how. We did not know each other; there was no way of determining that I would not hurt her. There was no reason why she should trust me and she was not going to. Such a courageous little being to face up to all of us, who were so much bigger and stronger and more powerful, to face us unflinchingly, without words or tears.

I inched closer. We had been there waiting at least a half hour. I was within ten feet of her now and she was beginning to view my approach with suspicion. I stopped moving. All the while I spoke in gentle tones, reassuring her that I meant her no harm, that we would go back to the classroom together, that nothing would happen. I spoke of other things too; things the children liked to do in our room; things we enjoyed doing together; things she would do with us.

Endless minutes passed. I was getting sore from not moving. Her legs were shaking from standing so long

35

without shifting position. This had become a test of endurance. An eternity was strung out over the ten feet separating us.

We waited. The frenzy was fading from her eyes. Tiredness was taking over. I wondered what the time was but was afraid to move my arm to see my watch. Still we waited.

The front of her overalls darkened and a puddle of urine formed around her feet. She looked down at it, taking her eyes from me for the first time. She caught her lower lip in her teeth. When she looked up, the horror of what had just happened showed plainly.

"Accidents happen. You haven't had a chance to go to the bathroom, so it really isn't your fault," I said. It amazed me that after the havoc she had wreaked in the classroom, this was the act that caused her regret.

"We can clean it up," I suggested. "I've got some rags back in the room for when this sort of thing happens."

She looked down again and then back at me. I remained silent. She took a cautious step backwards to better survey the situation. "You gonna whip me?" she asked hoarsely.

"No. I don't whip kids."

Her brow furrowed.

"I'll help you clean it up. We won't have to tell anybody. It can be our secret, because I know it was an accident."

"I didn't mean to."

"I know it."

"You gonna whip me?"

My shoulders dropped in exasperation. "No, Sheila, I don't whip kids. I said that to you once."

She looked at her overalls. "My Pa, he gonna whip me fierce when he sees I do this."

Throughout our exchange I had remained motionless in my spot, fearful of breaking this tenuous relationship. "We'll take care of that, don't worry. We've still got a while before school is over. It'll dry by then."

She rubbed her nose and looked at the puddle and then at me. For the first time since she'd arrived, she seemed uncertain. Very slowly I rose to my feet. She took a step backwards. I extended an arm to her. "Come on, we'll go get something to clean it up. Don't worry about it."

For a long moment she regarded me. Then cautiously she came toward me. She refused my hand but walked back to the classroom at my side.

Things had quieted in the room. Anton and the children were singing songs. Whitney was holding Susannah and Mary was rocking Max. The dead fish were all gone. Heads turned toward us but I motioned to Anton to keep them busy. Sheila accepted the rags and bucket from me and we went back to the gym and cleaned the floor without speaking. Then she followed me back to the room.

Surprisingly the remainder of the afternoon went quietly. The children were all subdued, fearful of toppling their frail control again. Sheila retreated to the chair she had occupied all morning, folded herself up in it and sucked her thumb. She did not move for the rest of the afternoon. Yet she continued to watch us. Her eyes were unreadable. I went around to each of the children and cuddled them and talked with them trying to soothe their unworded feelings. Finally I came to Sheila.

Sitting down on the floor beside her chair, I looked up at her. She regarded me seriously, thumb still in her mouth. The toll of the afternoon showed on her. I made no attempt to touch her. Anton was conducting the closing exercises and no one was watching us. I did not want to spook her by being too intimate, but I did want her to know I cared.

"It's been kind of a hard afternoon, hasn't it?" I said. She did not respond other than staring at me. I got the full benefit of her odor from this position. "Tomorrow will be better, I think. First days are always hard." I tried to read her eyes, to glean some understanding of what was going on in her head. The open hostility was gone, momentarily at least. But I could see nothing beyond that. "Are your pants dry?"

She unfolded and stood up, inspecting them. They were passably dry, the damp outline barely distinguishable from the other filth. She nodded slightly.

"Is that going to be good enough so you don't get in trouble?"

Again an almost imperceptible nod.

"I hope so. Everybody has accidents. And this wasn't

37

really your fault. You didn't have a chance to use the bathroom." I kept some spare clothes around because this sort of thing happened all too frequently in our room. I hadn't mentioned it, being afraid of frightening her with too much familiarity. But I wanted her to know that such problems were acceptable in here.

The thumb rotated in her mouth and she turned away from me to watch Anton. I remained near her until dismissal.

After the children were gone, Anton and I cleaned up the room in silence. Neither of us mentioned what had happened. Neither of us said much of anything. This certainly had not been one of our better days. When I got home after work, I washed out my pencil wound and put a Band-Aid on it. Then I lay down on my bed and wept.

CHAPTER 4

LIFE IN MY CLASSROOM WAS A CONSTANT
battle whether I wanted to acknowledge it or not. Not
only with the children but with myself. To cope with
these youngsters from day to day I locked up my own
emotions in many ways because I found that when I
didn't I became too discouraged, too shocked, too disil-
lusioned to function effectively. My days were a constant shooing of my own fears back into the little corners
where they dwelled. The method worked for me but
every once in a while a child came along who could
really rock my bulwark. Out came tumbling all the un-
certainties, the frustrations, and the misgivings I had
so carefully tried to ignore and I became overwhelmed
with defeat.

Basically, though, I was a dreamer. Beyond the children's incomprehensible behavior and my own vulner-
ability, beyond the discouragement, the self-doubts,
soared a dream which admittedly was seldom realized,
a dream that things could change. And being a dreamer,
my dream died hard.

This time was no exception. The tears were short-lived
and instead, I fell asleep. Later, I settled down with a

tuna fish sandwich to watch "Star Trek." I had never watched much television and had never seen "Star Trek" when it had been a prime-time program. But now, years later, it was shown in syndication each evening at six. At the beginning of the school year when our classroom adjustment had been slow to come and my disillusionments had been many, I had started watching the program while I ate dinner and it had become a ritual. It divided my day into the work part and the rest part; that hour being the recuperative time when I put away all the problems and frustrations that had occurred at school. Marvelously emotionless Mr. Spock became my after-work martini.

So by the time Chad arrived at seven, I had recovered. Chad and I had been seeing each other regularly over the previous eighteen months. At first it had been the typical courting relationship: the endless rounds of dinner, movies, dances and mindless conversation. However, neither of us was suited for that sort of affair. So we drifted into a warm, comfortable alliance. Chad was a junior partner in a law firm downtown and spent most of his time as a court-appointed attorney for the drifters and ne'er-do-wells who found themselves in jail. Consequently he did not have a good track record of winning cases. So we would spend our evenings together commiserating good-naturedly over my kids and his clients. We had talked once or twice about marriage, but that had been the extent of it. Both of us were sociable loners, satisfied with the status quo.

When Chad came over, bringing a quart of Baskin-Robbins chocolate fudge ice cream, I told him about Sheila as we fixed sundaes. I had met my match, I stated firmly. The kid was a savage and I did not think I was the one to civilize her. The sooner the opening at the hospital came up, the better.

Chad laughed amiably and suggested I call her former teacher. After our ice cream orgy when I was feeling comfortably full and a little more mellow about things, I looked in the telephone book for Mrs. Barthuly.

"Oh my gosh," Mrs. Barthuly said when I told her who I was and why I had called. "I thought they had put her away for good."

I explained that there had been no openings yet at the

40

state hospital and asked her what she had done while Sheila was in her class. I could hear her making little clucking sounds, those indescribable little noises of defeat.

"I've never seen such a child. Destructive, oh my gosh, every time I took my eyes off her she destroyed something. Her work, the other children's work, bulletin boards, art displays, anything. One time she took all the other kids' coats and stuffed them down the toilets in the girls' lavatory. Flooded the entire basement." She sighed. "I tried everything to stop her. She always destroyed her work before you could get a look at it. I started laminating the work-sheets so she couldn't tear them up. You know what she did? She shoved them into the cooling system and jammed the air conditioner. We went three days with no ventilation when it was ninety-four degrees."

Mrs. Barthuly went on to describe event after event. Her voice was rapid at first as if she had never had an adequate opportunity to tell about the chaos visited on her the first three months of the school year. But then it began to take on a weary note. Despite everything, she had liked Sheila, drawn by the same enigmatic force that had attracted me. The child seemed so vulnerable and still so brave. She had wanted to do right by Sheila. But nothing she did helped. Sheila refused to speak to her. She refused to be touched, to be helped, to be liked. In the beginning Mrs. Barthuly had tried to be kind. She attempted to show affection to this unlovable child, to include her in special activities, to give her extra attention. The school psychologist had set up behavior-management programs to reward Sheila's good behavior. But Sheila appeared to delight in never doing whatever it was they decided to reward. Mrs. Barthuly was convinced that Sheila purposely set out to ruin the programs, going so far as to stop doing some things she had previously been doing well when those things were included on the program.

Next, Mrs. Barthuly tried controlling her outlandish behavior negatively. She took away privileges, confined her to a time-out corner, and at last ended up sending Sheila to the principal for paddling. Still Sheila continued to terrorize the class, attacking other children, destroy-

41

ing things and refusing to work. At last, Mrs. Barthuly gave up. This child took too much time away from the other children. So Sheila was left on her own and the first semblance of peace settled in the room. Allowed to do as she pleased, Sheila spent most of the day wandering around the classroom or paging through magazines. If countered, Sheila would scream and tear about in revenge, destroying whatever was in her path. However, left entirely alone, she was tolerable and would ignore the others if they ignored her. She still never spoke, never did any work, nor participated in any classroom activities. Then the event in November occurred and she was removed immediately from school in response to fears expressed by other children's parents.

The voice on the other end of the phone was sad and pessimistic. Mrs. Barthuly regretted that so little had been done. No one knew if Sheila had even the most basic command of letters or numbers. Nothing about the child's learning or feelings was known at all. She was, Mrs. Barthuly admitted, the closest thing to an unteachable child she had ever encountered. Whatever could be done for Sheila was beyond her patience, ability and time. She wished me luck, amending it to say she hoped the state hospital placement came through soon. Then she hung up.

The news filled me with renewed depression because I did not know what I could do that had not been tried. With my group of children, I did not have much more of a chance to give her one-to-one attention than Mrs. Barthuly. I discussed the matter with Chad and decided there was nothing I could do other than wait and see.

The next morning before school, Anton and I sat down to plan our course of action. Clearly the occurrence which had happened the day before could not be repeated. The other children could not afford to go through that sort of experience. Some disruption was healthy in the classroom because it taught them how to respond in a supportive environment when things went wrong; but we could not afford chaos for days on end.

The social worker came in dragging Sheila about fifteen minutes before class started. She explained that the only bus they could get to connect with Sheila's home was the high school bus. Therefore, Sheila would be arriving each day a half hour early and would not be able to catch the bus home in the evening until two hours after class had finished. I was horrified. First of all, I did not feel Sheila was in any shape to be riding a bus with a bunch of high school kids; I doubted seriously that she could be trusted on any bus. Second, what was I supposed to do with her for two hours after school? The mere thought had frozen my stomach into a cold, iron-heavy lump.

The social worker smiled blankly. We would have to go along with the idea because the school district would not pay for special transportation when existing buses could be used. Arrangements would simply have to be made for her to stay at school. Other buses out to the country came almost as late and other children had to be waiting somewhere in the school. Sheila could wait with them. Transferring Sheila's limp wrist to me, she turned and left.

I looked down at Sheila and felt all my anxiety from the day before flood over me. She was regarding me, her eyes round and guarded, the hostility more hidden than the day before. I smiled weakly. "Good morning, Sheila. I'm glad you're with us again today."

In the few moments we had before the other children all arrived, I brought Sheila over to one of the tables and pulled a chair out for her. She had come with me from the door without protest and sat in the chair. "Listen," I said, sitting down next to her, "let's get an idea about what's going to happen in here today so we won't have another one like yesterday. That wasn't very much fun for me, and I don't suppose it was for you either."

Her brow wrinkled in a questioning expression as if she did not understand what I was doing.

"I don't know how it was for you at your other school, but I want you to know how it's going to be in here. Yesterday, I think we may have scared you a little bit, because you didn't know any of us and it might not have been clear what we expected. So, I'm going to tell you."

She began hunching herself up into the chair, drawing her knees up and folding in upon herself again. I noticed that she was still wearing the same worn denim

43

overalls and T-shirt. Neither had been washed since yesterday and she smelled very strongly.

"I'm not going to hurt you. I don't hurt kids in here. Neither does Anton or Whitney or anyone else. You don't have to be frightened of us."

The thumb was in her mouth. She seemed scared of me and looked so little and vulnerable, making it difficult for me to remember her as she had been yesterday. The bravado was gone, at least temporarily. But her gaze remained unflinching as she watched me.

"Would you like to sit in my lap while I talk to you?" She shook her head almost imperceptibly.

"Okay, well, here's the plan. I want you to join us when we do things. All you have to do is sit with us. Anton or Whitney or I will help you find out what is happening until you get used to it." I went ahead to explain the day's schedule. I told her she did not have to participate if she did not want to, just yet. But she did have to join us and there was no choice on that. Either she came of her own accord or one of us would help her.

"And," I concluded, "sometimes when things get out of control, the place I will have you go is over to the quiet corner." I indicated our chair in the corner. "You go and you sit there until both of us think you have things under control again. You just sit, that's all. Is that clear?"

If it was, she did not let me know. By that point the others were arriving. I rose and patted her on the back before going to greet the other children. She did not pull away from my touch but then she did not acknowledge it either.

When morning discussion came, Sheila was still sitting in the chair. I pointed to the floor beside me. "Sheila, over here, please, so we can start discussion."

She did not move. I repeated myself. Still she remained folded up in the chair. I could feel my stomach tighten in anticipation. She regarded me, her thumb in her mouth, her eyes wide. I looked to Anton, who was settling Freddie into place. "Anton, would you help Sheila join us?"

When Anton turned to approach her, Sheila came to life and bolted off the chair. She made a mad dash for the door, falling hard against it when the latch did not respond.

"Torey, make her stop," Peter said worriedly. The other children were watching Anton as he circled to catch her. She had that trapped-animal stare again and was dashing recklessly about trying to avoid capture. But the room was so small it was a futile flight. She attempted to deter him by knocking books off the counters but within a minute Anton had her cornered on the far side of one of the tables. Briefly, they danced back and forth, but Anton unexpectedly shoved the table toward her pinning her against the wall just long enough to reach and catch hold of her arm.

For the first time she made a sound. She let loose with a scream that startled all of us. Susannah began to cry, but the others sat in fearful silence while Anton wrestled Sheila over to the group. I remained sitting and pointed to the spot I had indicated earlier. Taking her by the arm from Anton I pushed her into a sitting position. She continued to scream, a throaty, tearless yell, but she sat without struggling.

"Okay," I said with fake brightness. "Who has a topic?"

"I do," said William, straining to be heard over Sheila's screams. "Is it always going to be like this in here?" His dark eyes were fearful. "Is she always going to be like this?"

The other children were watching me anxiously, and I realized, not for the first time, what a con job my position was, because I was honestly as frightened as they were. We had been together four months and had learned each other's differences and problems. I knew Sheila would have been hard on us even if she had been quiet and cooperative, simply because she was new, testing our tenuous hold on order. But she was in no way easy to accept and she shook us all to our foundation.

So the topic that day was Sheila. I tried to explain as best I could that Sheila was adjusting and like all the rest of us was having a hard time. She simply needed our patience and understanding.

Sheila was not entirely ignoring us as we discussed her. Her screaming had diminished to sporadic squawks, inserted when there was too great a gap in our conversation or when one of us looked at her and she caught us

45

at it. Otherwise, she was quiet. I let the children ask questions and express their fears and unhappiness. And I attempted to answer them honestly. All except Peter had the sensitivity not to be too critical in front of Sheila. Peter did not. Like the day before when he had complained of her smell, he angrily stated that he wanted this girl out of his room. She was ruining everything. I did not attempt to protect Sheila from his comments because I knew he would make them to her later anyway. That was all part of Peter's own problems and I preferred to be present when he talked.

So instead we discussed alternate ways of dealing with the inconveniences put upon us while Sheila adjusted. Tyler suggested sending her to the quiet corner to save our ears. Sarah opted to get freetime every time Sheila started a ruckus. And Guillermo, who seemed to be feeling particularly magnanimous, thought the children might take turns sitting with Sheila and keeping her company while she hollered so she wouldn't get lonely. I suspected he was reflecting more on his own feelings than on Sheila's.

In the end we decided that when Sheila yelled or in other ways demanded Anton's or my attention and disrupted the class, the other kids were to get busy at their own work and the more responsible ones were to keep an eye on Max and Freddie and Susannah. I told them that at the end of the week we would have a treat if everyone cooperated. After a short discussion we decided that we would make ice cream on Friday if everything worked out. The children were full of ideas.

"If you get busy with Sheila and Freddie starts crying, I can read him a story," Tyler suggested.

"We could sing a song by ourselves," Guillermo added.

"I'll hold Susannah Joy's hand so she won't run and hurt herself."

I smiled. "Everybody's got good ideas. This is going to work out real well, I can tell. So you just think what kind of ice cream topping you want on Friday." I looked down at Sheila, who was still making angry grunts. I continued hanging on to one overall strap, but she was sitting peacefully. "Do you like ice cream?"

She narrowed her eyes.

"I expect you'll want some, won't you? Do you like ice cream?"

Cautiously she nodded.

Sheila was more cooperative about moving to a chair while we had math. She climbed on one and folded herself up, watching me suspiciously as I went from child to child. The rest of the morning passed uneventfully.

I did not dare let lunch follow as it had the previous day, not only because I did not want a replay of the disastrous afternoon, but because the lunch aides had stated that they unequivocally refused to supervise her until she was more predictable. So I took my lunch and ate with the children.

I sat next to Sheila, who inched away from me on the cafeteria bench. Anton came and sat down on the other side of her and she inched back in my direction. She bolted her lunch down in minutes by cramming it into her mouth as fast as she could chew. Her manners were atrocious, but she could maneuver a fork, which was more than some of the others could manage.

After lunch I escorted her back to the room, sat down at one of the tables and graded papers while the children played. Sheila resumed her seat on the chair, put her thumb in her mouth and stared at me.

All afternoon she moved as requested, although when given a choice she always returned to the same chair at the table and hunched up on it. She appeared considerably subdued from the day before, almost depressed, but I made no attempt to question her. She seemed unduly frightened of me, which I did not understand, so I did not want to intensify her concerns by forcing myself upon her. The other children seemed disappointed that nothing happened and Peter came up to me after closing exercises to ask if we would still have ice cream if Sheila never misbehaved again. With a grin I assured him that if we went all the way to Friday with no problems, there would certainly be ice cream.

After the other children left, we were alone, Sheila, Anton and I. Those two hours after school were normally my preparation time for the next day, but I thought that perhaps for the first few days at least, I might use them to get better acquainted with Sheila. She

47

still sat in her chair, having not even gotten up when the other children put on their snowsuits and prepared to go home.

I came over to the table and sat down across from her. She regarded me, her eyes wary. "You did a nice job today, scout. I really liked that."

She averted her face.

I looked at her. Under the dirt and tangles was a handsome child. Her limbs were straight and well-formed. I longed to hold her, to take her in my lap and hug away some of that pain so obvious in her eyes. But we remained a table apart, which might as well have been a universe. With me so close, she would not even meet my eyes.

"Have I frightened you, Sheila?" I asked softly. "I didn't mean to, if I did. It must be very scary for you, having to come to a new school and be with all of us when you don't know us. I know that's scary. It scares me too."

She put her hand up to the side of her face to block me entirely from view.

"Would you like me to read you a story or something while we wait for your bus?"

She shook her head.

"All right. Well, I'm going to go over to the other table and make plans for tomorrow. If you change your mind, I'll be glad to read to you. Or you play with the toys or whatever you like." I rose from the table.

As soon as I had settled at my work she put her hand down and turned to me, studying me as I wrote. I looked up a few times but there was no response from that steady gaze.

CHAPTER 5

THE NEXT DAY I DECIDED IT WAS TIME FOR Sheila to participate. The bus which brought her dropped her off at the high school two blocks away, so Anton had gone to get her and walk her to our school. When they arrived, Sheila pulled off her jacket and went straight to her chair. I came over and sat down, explaining that to-day she was going to be asked to do some things. I went over the schedule of the day with her and told her I expected her to join us for everything just like the day before, and that I also expected her to work some math problems for me at math time. Also on Wednesday after-noons we always cooked, I said, so I wanted her to help us make chocolate bananas. Those two things she was expected to do.

She watched me as I spoke, her eyes clouded with the same distrust they had shown the day before. I asked if she understood what I wanted. She did not respond.

During morning discussion Sheila joined us when re-quested after I gave her the evil eye. She sat at my feet and did nothing. Math was a different story. I had planned to do some simple counting exercises using manipulatives. So I got out the blocks and called her to come over to me. She remained sitting in the spot where she had been for morning discussion.

"Sheila, come over here, please." I indicated a chair. It was the one she was so fond of. "Come on."

She did not move. Anton began to move cautiously to catch her if she bolted when I approached. Instantly she perceived our plan and panicked. This child was phobic about being chased. Shrieking wildly, she darted off, knocking children and their work over as she fled. But Anton was too close and snagged her almost immediately. I came in and took her from him.

"Honey, we're not going to do anything to you when we come to get you. Don't you know that?" I sat down with her, holding her tightly as she struggled and listening to her breathing, raspy with fear. "Take it easy, kitten."

"Hey, everybody," Peter hollered delightedly, "everybody be good now." Little heads bent eagerly over their work and Tyler rose solicitously to check on Susannah and Max.

Sheila resumed screaming, her face reddening. But she did not cry. Holding her in my lap, I spilled out the counting blocks. I lined them up evenly while waiting for her to calm down. "Here, I want you to count some blocks for me."

She yelled louder.

"Here, count three out for me." She struggled to break my hold. "I'll help you." I manipulated a writhing hand toward the blocks. "One, two, three. There. Now you try."

Unexpectedly she grabbed a block and hurled it across the room. Within a split second she had another which hit Tyler squarely in the forehead. Tyler let out a wail.

I pinned Sheila's arm to her side and stood up, lugging her over to the quiet corner. "We don't do that in here. Nobody is hurt in here. I want you to sit in the chair until you quiet down and can come back and work." I motioned Anton over. "Help her stay in the chair if she needs it."

I returned to the other children, rubbed Tyler's sore spot and praised everybody for keeping busy. Putting a check on the board to indicate our approach toward

Friday's ice cream, I then settled in next to Freddie to help him stack blocks. Over in the corner all hell had broken loose. Sheila shrieked wildly, kicking the wall with her tennis shoes and bouncing the chair. Anton was grimly silent, holding her firmly in place.

Throughout math period Sheila continued the ruckus. By the time free play had started half an hour later, she was tiring of kicking and fighting. I came over.

"Are you ready to come do your math with me?" I asked. She looked up at me and screamed wordlessly in anger. Anton was no longer holding on to her, just to the chair, and I motioned him away to keep an eye on the others. "When you are ready for math, you may come over. Until then I want you in the chair." Then I turned and left.

Leaving her entirely alone startled her momentarily and she stopped yelling. When she became fully aware that neither Anton nor I was standing over her to keep her in the chair, she stood up.

"Are you ready to do math?" I asked from across the room where I was helping Peter build a highway out of blocks.

Her face blackened with my question. "No! No! No! No!"

"Then sit back down."

She screeched in rage, her sudden change in volume causing everyone to pause. But she remained beside the chair.

"I said sit down, Sheila. You may not get up until you're ready to do math."

For an eternal moment she stormed with so much loudness I felt my head pulse. Then suddenly, startlingly, everything was quiet and she glowered at me. Such obvious hate withered what little self-confidence I had about what I was doing.

"Sit down in that chair, Sheila."

She sat. She turned the chair around so she could watch me, but she sat. Then she resumed screaming. I sighed a deep, private sigh of relief.

Peter looked at me. "You know, Torey, I think we ought to get two marks for good behavior on this one. She's pretty hard to ignore."

51

I grinned. "Yeah, Peter, I think you're right. This is worth two."

Sheila screamed and yelled all through playtime. The ruckus had been going over an hour and a half by then. She stomped her feet and bounced and rocked the chair. She pulled at her clothes and shook her fists. But she remained in the chair.

By snacktime she was hoarse and all that came from the corner was little strangled croaks. But her rage had not diminished and the croaks continued furiously. I stayed inside while Anton took the others out for recess. This increased Sheila's agitation for a few moments and she gasped out a few more shouts and rattled the chair around. But she was tiring. By the end of recess there were no sounds at all coming from the corner. My head was throbbing.

I did not restate the conditions for leaving the corner. I believed she was bright enough to know by that time and I did not want to give her added attention. The other children came in, frosty and red-cheeked from recess, full of tales about playing fox-and-geese in the snow with Anton, who got caught every time. Reading period started without event, all of us settling down to our tasks as if the little lump on the chair in the corner did not exist.

Toward the close of the period I felt a feather-light touch on my shoulder as I worked with Max. I turned to see Sheila standing behind me, her skin mottled with her anxiety, her face puckered with that cautious expression so frequently reflected in her eyes.

"You ready to do math?"

She pursed her lips a moment and then nodded slowly.

"Okay. Let me get Sarah to help Max. You go over and pick up the blocks you threw and get the others out of the cupboard by the sink." I spoke in a casual, offhanded manner as if it were normal to expect her to comply, my tight chest belying the degree of the con. She looked at me carefully but then went and did as I had asked.

Together we sat down on the floor and I spilled out the blocks. "Show me three blocks."

Cautiously she picked out three.

"Show me ten." Again, ten cubes were lined up on the rug before me. "Good girl. You know your numbers well, don't you?"

She looked up anxiously.

"I'm going to make it harder. Count mè out twenty-seven." Within seconds twenty-seven blocks appeared.

"Can you add?"

She did not respond.

"Show me how many blocks are two plus two." Four blocks appeared without hesitation. I studied her a moment. "How about three plus five?" She laid out eight cubes.

I could not tell if she actually knew the answers or was solving them as she went along. Yet she clearly understood the mechanics behind adding. I was reluctant to get out pencil and paper, knowing her tendency to destroy paper. I did not want to ruin our fragile, newly won relationship. But I did want to know how she was working the problems. So I decided to switch to subtraction, which would tell me more. "Show me three take away one."

Sheila flipped two blocks out. I smiled. That problem she obviously knew without having to place three blocks out and remove one.

"Do six take away four."

Again two cubes.

"Hey, you're pretty smart. But I've got one for you. I'll get you this time. Show me twelve take away seven."

She looked up at me and the very smallest hint of a smile colored her eyes although it did not touch her lips. She stacked one, two, three, four, five blocks on top of one another. She did it without even looking down at the cubes. The little devil, I thought. Wherever she had been these past few years and whatever she had been doing, she was also learning. Her abilities were better than the average child her age. She gave no indication of even hesitating before laying the blocks out. My heart leaped at the possibility of having a bright child under all that protest and grime.

She did a few more problems for me before I said enough and she could put the blocks away. It was reading period now and I had told her in the morning that she did not have to participate in this activity. I rose to

53

check on the other kids and Sheila rose with me. Still clutching the box of blocks she wandered after me.

"Honey," I said turning to her, "you can put those away, if you want. You don't have to carry them around."

Sheila had other ideas. The next time I looked up, she was in her favorite chair at the other end of the table with the blocks spilled before her. Busily she was manipulating them, doing something, but I could not tell what.

Lunch subdued her again and she retreated to hunching up in the chair. But when it came time to cook, I coaxed her off quite easily with a banana on a Popsicle stick.

Every Wednesday we made something to eat. I had done it for a variety of reasons. For the more controlled kids, it was a good exercise in math and reading. For everyone it encouraged social activity, sharing, conversation and mutual work. Moreover, cooking was fun. Once a month we repeated a favorite recipe that the kids had chosen and this afternoon it was chocolate bananas, a messy affair involving a banana stuck on a stick that was dipped into chocolate and rolled in topping and then frozen. I had decided not to tackle a new recipe on Sheila's first day out to simplify things, and chocolate bananas were a popular standby. Almost all the kids could manage all the parts by themselves. Even Susannah could do most of it, leaving only Max and Freddie to supervise carefully. Naturally, there was chocolate everywhere and a good share of the toppings were eaten before they found a banana to adhere to, but we all had a marvelous time.

Sheila hesitated to join in, clutching her banana tightly and watching from the sidelines as the others babbled gaily. Yet, she was not resistant and Whitney lured her over to the chocolate sauce when everyone else had finished. Once Sheila started, she became fully absorbed and began trying to roll all four different toppings onto her sticky banana. I watched from the far side of the table. She never spoke but it became apparent she had some definite ideas about how to get the toppings to stick by redipping the banana in the chocolate after each roll in a topping. One by one the other children

54

began pausing to watch her as she experimented with her idea. Voices became hushed as curiosity got the better of them. Rolling the huge, sticky mass in the last dish of topping, she lifted it up carefully. Her eyes rose to meet mine and slowly a smile spread across her face until it was broad and open, showing the gaps where her bottom teeth were missing.

At the end of each day we had closing exercises which, like morning topic were designed to unite us and prepare us for our time apart. One of the activities was the Kobold's Box. I loved to make up stories to tell the children and had once told them back at the beginning of the year that kobolds were like fairies, but that they lived in people's houses and watched over them to keep things safe while people slept. Peter had suggested that there might be a kobold in our room who took care of all our things and kept Benny, Charles and Onions, the bad-tempered rabbit, company during the night. This spawned a number of tales about our kobold. So one day I brought a large wooden box and told the kids that this was where the kobold was going to leave messages. I said he had watched all of us at work and had been extremely pleased with how kind and thoughtful everyone in the room was becoming. Therefore, every time he saw a kind deed done, he would leave a message in the box. So during closing exercises each day, I read the notes from the Kobold's Box. After a few days I told them the kobold was getting writer's cramp and needed a helping hand because so many people were being kind. I asked the children to be on the lookout for others doing kind things and to write a note and put it in the box, or if they could not write, to come to me and I would write it for them. Thus, one of our most popular and effective exercises occurred. Every night there were about thirty notes from the kids to each other over perceived kindnesses. This not only encouraged the children to observe positive behaviors in others, but they also knocked each other over being kind in hopes that their names would appear in the box at the end of the day. Some notes were traditional but others showed particular insight praising a child for small but significant steps, sometimes for things I myself had missed. For instance,

55

Sarah was complimented for not using a particularly favorite vulgar phrase during an argument one day, and Freddie was praised for finding a Kleenex instead of blowing his nose on his shirt. I loved opening that box every night because I seldom contributed to it myself except to make sure everybody had at least one note. The thrill of seeing what the children had perceived was so exciting to me. And admittedly, I also enjoyed finding a note for myself in there.

So closing exercises after cooking on Wednesday were particularly fun because for the first time Sheila's name appeared in handwriting other than my own. Sheila who still sat apart from us kept her head down when the kids clapped over her notes. But she accepted the notes readily when I gave them to her.

Anton walked the other children out to their buses after school ended. I settled down at the table to grade papers and to bring some behavioral charts I was keeping on a couple of the kids up to date. Sheila had gone into the bathroom to clean the final dregs of the chocolate banana from her face. She had been in there some time and I had become involved in my work. I heard the toilet flush and she came out. I did not look up because I was completing a graph with marking pen and did not want to make an error. Sheila came over to the table and watched me a moment. Then she came closer, putting her elbows on the table and leaning way over so that we were only inches apart. I raised my eyes to look at her. She examined my face thoughtfully.

"How come them other kids don't go to the bathroom in the toilet?"

"Huh?" I sat back in surprise.

"I say, how come them other kids, them big kids, go in their pants and not in the toilet?"

"Well, that's something they haven't learned yet."

"How come? They do be big kids. Bigger than me."

"Well, they just haven't learned it yet. But we're working on it. Everyone's trying."

She looked down at the graph I was drawing. "They oughta know that by now. My Pa, he'd whip me fierce bad if I do that."

"Everybody's different and nobody gets a whipping in here."

She was pensive a long moment. She traced a little circle on the table with her finger. "This here be a crazy class, don't it?"

"Not really, Sheila."

"My Pa, he say so. He say I be crazy and they put me in a class for crazy kids. He says this here be a crazy kidses class."

"Not really."

She frowned a moment. "I don't care much. This here do be as good as that other place I be before. It be as good as anyplace. I don't care if it be a crazy class."

I was at a loss for words, not knowing how to deny the obvious. I had not expected to be involved with one of my children in this sort of discussion. Most were either not coherent enough to be that perceptive or not brash enough to say it.

Sheila scratched her head and regarded me thoughtfully. "Do you be crazy?"

I laughed. "I hope not."

"How come you do this?"

"What? Work here? Because I like boys and girls a lot and I think that teaching is fun."

"How come you be with crazy kids?"

"I like it. Being crazy isn't bad. It's just different, that's all."

She shook her head without smiling and straightened up. "I think you do be a crazy person too."

CHAPTER 6

"SHEILA, COME OVER HERE, PLEASE," I MOtioned to a chair near where I was sitting. "I have something for you to do." Sheila sat across the room in her favorite chair. Thus far, the morning had gone smoothly. Like the previous two days, I had used the time before school to tell her what would happen that day. She had been cooperative, joining us for morning discussion without being reminded, and then for math. Although she still did not speak, she appeared considerably more relaxed in the classroom. Now she watched me from her chair.

"Come here, hon. I want you to do something with me." I beckoned to her. She unfolded from her post hesitantly. I had borrowed a test from the school psychologist called a Peabody Picture Vocabulary Test or more affectionately the PPVT. Although I never cared much for the test, it gave a general idea of a child's functioning verbal IQ quickly and without the child needing to talk. After the previous day's encounter with the math cubes, I was intensely interested to know the level at which the girl was functioning. With such a severe disturbance as Sheila displayed, it was typical for her to be academically behind. Most seriously disturbed children simply do not have the extra energy available to learn. So when she evidenced normal math skill, I became alive with curiosity. I was also excited to think she might have above-average intelligence. I was already beginning to mellow about her placement in my room and wondering about keeping her out of the state hospital. Of all the things she needed right now, I realized that was not one of them.

"You and I are going to do something together." I had had to get up and bring her over to my table. "Here, sit down. Now, I'm going to show you some pictures and say a word. Then I want you to point to the picture that best shows what that word means, okay? Do you understand that?"

She nodded. I showed the first set of four pictures and asked her to point to "whip." What a picture to have to start with, I thought ruefully. She studied the four line drawings, looked up at me, then cautiously pointed to one.

"Good girl," I smiled at her. "That's just exactly right. Point to 'net.' "

As I read each word, Sheila would point to a picture, hesitantly at first, studying each of the four choices carefully, then more freely. After six or seven plates a small smile slipped across her face and she raised her eyes. "This be easy," she whispered hoarsely so the others could not hear.

She missed one, "thermos," a word she had probably not encountered in her short, destitute life. But the next one she did correctly. A child had to miss six out of eight to stop the test, and she gave no indication of reaching that level. We continued. The words were beginning to get harder and she was taking more time to consider the pictures. Occasionally she would miss one, sometimes two. I could see the concern in her eyes; she knew when she missed them, even if I made no comments.

I had stopped making comments some time back. I had suspected she was above average in intelligence, maybe even bright, but she had long since passed my expectations. We were moving into a part of the test I had never given before because none of my kids had ever gone that high. We were working with words like "illumination" and "concentric." Sheila was missing words regularly, but never six out of eight. Tension mounted around us. She was obviously trying very hard not to make mistakes and I was touched by her concentration. But we were up into the adolescent end of the test; there were words no normal six-year-old would know. Biting her lips between her teeth, she kept trying. In her lap, I could see her wringing her hands.

"Sweetheart, you're doing a nice job," I said. I hadn't expected her to take the test so seriously and become so involved, to try so hard and to last so long. I really could not believe she knew these words.

She looked up at me. Her eyes were dilated, the soft skin at her throat mottled with nervousness. "I ain't getting them all right."

"Oh, that's okay, honey. You aren't supposed to get them all right. These are words for great big kids and you're not expected to know them all. This is just to see which ones you do know. But it doesn't matter if you get some wrong. I'm proud of you for trying so hard."

Her face puckered and she looked on the verge of tears. "These be fierce hard words now." She looked down at her hands. "First they be easy, but these do be terrible hard for me. I don't know them all."

Her tiny voice, her slipping hold on her composure, her small shoulders hunched up under the worn shirt all combined to rip at my heart. Such innocence, even in the worst of these kids. They were all simply little children.

I reached an arm out. "Come here, Sheila." She looked up at me and I leaned over and pulled her up into my lap. Under my hands her little body was tense, the omnipresent odor of old urine floating around us. "Kitten, I know you're trying your best. That's all that counts. I don't really care which ones you get right or wrong, that doesn't matter. Why, these are really hard words. I bet there isn't another boy or girl in here who could do better."

I held her, smoothing back the tangled hair from her face. Waiting for her to relax I looked over the test score sheet, mentally subtracting out the errors. I suspected she was very close to reaching the ceiling of her ability on the

60

test. She was missing three and four at a time. But even so, she had surpassed any other child I had ever tested.

"How do you know all these words?" I asked, my curiosity getting the better of me.

She shrugged. "I dunno."

"Some of these are big kids' words. I just wondered where you heard them."

"My other teacher, she let me have magazines. Sometimes I read the words in there."

I looked down at her. Her body was still rigid against mine and light as that of a little bird. "Can you read, Sheila?"

She nodded.

"Where'd you learn to do that?"

"I dunno. I always read."

I shook my head in amazement. What sort of changeling did we have here? At first I had been titillated by the thought of a bright child, because as dear as the others were, most were slow learners and it was always hard to know where the disturbance left off and the retardation began. Some, like Sarah and Peter, were average, but I had seldom had an above-average child. At first, the thought had excited me. But clearly Sheila was not simply above average. She was way beyond the comfortableness that came with easy learning and mastery. Instead, she had been catapulted into that little-known realm of true giftedness. I feared that fact would not ease my job at all.

There was no scale to measure Sheila's score on the PPVT. For her age group the scale stopped at 99, which translated into a 170 IQ. Sheila had a score of 102. I stared at the test sheet. We don't have a concept for that kind of brilliance. Statistics tell us that less than 1 in 10,000 has that high a level of functioning. But what does it mean? It is a deviant score, an abnormality in a society that worships sameness. It would set her apart as surely as her disturbance could.

I looked across the room to where Sheila sat. It was playtime now and Sheila had resumed her favorite chair. I looked at her as she sat, thumb in mouth, limbs wrapped around herself protectively. She was watching Tyler and

61

Sarah, who were playing with dolls in the housekeeping corner. I wondered. Under that long matted hair, behind those wary eyes, what kind of child was there? I now felt more concerned than ever before, because if anything, the situation had become more complicated.

After lunch I showed Anton the test. He shook his head in disbelief. "That can't be right," he muttered. "Where would she learn those words? She just had to guess lucky, Torey. No kid in the migrant camp is going to know those kinds of words."

I could not believe it myself. So I put in a call to Allan, our school psychologist. He was out of the office but I left a message with his secretary saying I had a child that I wanted tested.

One thing from the testing situation puzzled me. As Sheila spoke to me more, it became increasingly apparent that she used a highly idiosyncratic dialect. I hadn't heard her enough to pick out the unusual features precisely, but the grammar was bizarre. Most of the migrant camp children came from Spanish-speaking homes and often their command of English vocabulary was below age-level but within normal limits grammatically. There was no other major speech variation in the locality. Sheila was not from a Spanish-speaking home; the IQ test substantiated that there was nothing wrong at all with her vocabulary. I could not fathom why she spoke so oddly. To me her dialect almost sounded like the inner-city blacks I had worked with in Cleveland. But Sheila was not black and our small Iowa farming community was far from inner-city Cleveland. Perhaps it was a family speech pattern. I decided I would have to investigate because the phenomenon left me so perplexed.

The remainder of the day went uneventfully. I still made minimal requirements of Sheila. I wanted to give her ample time to adjust to us without taxing the other kids too much. After the first tumultuous days, this was a welcome relief. She moved willingly with us, but participated infrequently and only when coaxed. She would not talk to the other children or to Whitney. In most instances she would not speak to Anton or me unless we were quite isolated. Yet, she was peaceful, sitting in her chair when given the opportunity and watching us with guarded interest.

The next major step that had to be taken with Sheila concerned her hygiene. Every day she arrived in the same denim overalls and boy's T-shirt. Apparently, the clothes had never been washed from the first day she wore them and she reeked of urine. I suspected she wet the bed and dressed each morning without washing. Consequently, she was extremely unpleasant to be near for any length of time. Both Anton and I were used to the strong odors of unchanged pants, since Max, Freddie, and Susannah were all not reliably toilet trained. But Sheila was even stronger than we were accustomed to. Moreover, the plain everyday grime was crusted over her face and arms. When I had sent her in to wash off the chocolate from cooking the day before, there were lines on her forearms indicating how high she had washed. Those same lines were visible today. She had long hair that went halfway down her back in tangled strands. I had checked the first day for lice or mites. We had struggled twice with lice already and I was not game for another encounter. The second time I had ended up catching them myself and had been furious. Sheila did not appear to have any, although she did have impetigo around her mouth, which I hoped none of the other children would catch.

A school nurse came once a week for an afternoon. I had tried to send my children down. Most of them had had impetigo or rat bites or other evils of poverty. But I ended up getting the salve and Kwell shampoo from the nurse and taking care of the kids myself, simply because once a week on Thursday afternoons was not often enough to tend to all the problems.

I waited until all the children had left at the end of the day to tackle Sheila's hygienic needs. She had remained sitting in her chair while the others had gotten ready to go home. She was still sitting when I went to the cupboard and got out the combs and brushes I kept there. The night before I had stopped at the drugstore and bought a little package of hair clips.

"Sheila, come here," I said. "I got something for you."

She rose and came over. Her brow was furrowed with

63

wary interest. I handed her the sack. For a moment she just held it, looking at me quizzically. But I urged her to open it and she did. Taking the clips out she looked at them and then at me. Her forehead was still wrinkled in puzzlement.

"They're for you, sweetheart. I thought we could comb your hair out nice and put clips in it. Like I've got in mine." I showed her my hair.

She fingered the clips carefully through the plastic wrapping. With a frown she regarded me. "How come you do this?"

"Do what?"

"Be nice to me?"

I looked at her in disbelief. "Because I like you."

"Why? I be a crazy kid; I hurt your fishes. Why do you be nice to me?"

I smiled through my own perplexity. "I just wanted to, Sheila. That's all. I thought you might like something nice for your hair."

She continued to rub the clips through the wrapping, feeling the plastic shapes with her fingertips. "Ain't nobody give me nothing before. Ain't nobody be nice to me on purpose."

I stood watching her in bewilderment. There was nothing in my experience to relate to that. "Well, things are different in her, kiddo," was all I could reply.

I brushed the tangles out of her hair carefully. It took much longer than I had anticipated it would because I did not want to hurt her in any way. I was fearful of this fragile relationship we were forming, of accidentally harming it because we were from such different worlds. She sat very patiently clutching the clips in her hands but never taking them out of the wrapping. Over and over again she fingered them, but she would not open the package. Her hair was that fine, soft, impossibly straight hair that fortunately never tangles too badly. When brushed out, it hung down below her shoulder blades in a thick curtain. In front I combed her bangs. They were too long, falling into her eyes. She was a pretty girl with bold, well-formed features. With soap and water she would be even lovelier.

"There you are. Here, give me the clips and I'll put them in your hair."

She squashed the clips to her breast.

"Here, let's put them in your hair."

She shook her head.

"Don't you want them there?"

"Pa, he take them away from me."

"He wouldn't do that, would he? Just tell him that I gave them to you."

"He say I steal them. Nobody give me nothing before." She held on to the clips tightly, looking at the plastic bluebirds and ducks through the wrapping.

"Maybe for now, you can leave them at school until I get hold of your dad and tell him I gave them to you. How's that sound?"

"You fix my hair nice again?"

I nodded. "I'll fix it tomorrow morning when you come."

She looked at the clips a long moment and then hesitantly handed them to me. "Here. You keep them for me."

My heart thumped within my chest as I took the clips. It was so obvious how hard she was finding giving them back. At that moment Anton came into the room with an armload of dittos he had been running off. He reminded me that it was almost time for him to walk Sheila over to the high school to catch her bus. I was surprised that so much time had slipped by. We hadn't even gotten around to washing up and she did smell so terrible.

"Sheila," I asked, "do you get a chance to wash yourself at home?"

She shook her head. "We ain't got no bathtub."

"Can you use the sink?"

"Ain't got no sink either. My Pa, he brings us down water in a bucket from the gas station." She paused staring at the floor. "It just be to drink out of. He'd be fierce awful mad at me if I get it dirty."

"Do you have any other clothes?"

She shook her head.

"Well, I'll tell you what. We'll see what we can do about that tomorrow, okay?"

Nodding she went to the coat hook to find her thin cotton jacket. I sighed as I watched her. So much to do, I thought. So much to change. "Good-bye, Sheila. Have a nice evening. I'll see you tomorrow."

Anton took her hand and opened the door into the blowy January darkness. Just as he was shutting the door behind him, Sheila paused, peering under his arm and toward me. She smiled slightly. "Bye, teacher."

CHAPTER 7

THE NEXT MORNING I CAME READY FOR AC-
tion. Armed with three bath towels, a bar of soap, shampoo and a bottle of baby lotion, I arrived at school. First
I went down to check the church box in the office. Although the school I was in was in one of the upper-income
areas, enough children like those in my room were bussed
in to warrant a box of spare clothes that could be given
away. I kept my own box in my room, but primarily it
contained underwear. What was in there was far too large
for little Sheila. Having found a pair of corduroy pants
and another T-shirt, I went back to my room.

Thus when Sheila arrived, I was running water into the
sink in the back of the classroom. The sink was a large,
roomy, kitchen-sized sink and I figured I would get a
good share of her into it, since we lacked shower facilities.
The moment she saw me, Sheila yanked off her jacket
and came trotting over. That was the fastest I had seen
her move toward me since she had come. Her eyes were
wide with interest as she leaned over to see what I was
doing. "You gonna put clips in my hair now?"

"You bet. But first we're going to give you the full

beauty-shop routine. We're going to wash you top to bottom. How does that sound?"

"It gonna hurt?"

I laughed. "No, silly. I don't think so."

She had pulled the bottle of baby lotion out of the bucket I had it in and she removed the top. "What do this be for? Do you eat it?"

I looked at her in surprise. "No, it's lotion. You put it on your body."

A sudden look of pleasure rippled across her face. "It do smell good, teacher. Smell it. It smell good and you put it on to be pretty smelling." Her eyes were animated. "Now that kid, he ain't gonna say I stink no more, huh?"

I smiled at her. "No, I guess he won't. Look here, I found some clothes for you to wear. Then Whitney can take your overalls over to the Laundromat when she comes this afternoon."

Sheila surveyed the corduroy pants, picking them up gingerly. "My Pa, he ain't gonna let me keep them. We don't take no charity things."

"Yes, I understand that. You just wear them until the others get dry. Okay?"

I lifted Sheila up onto the counter beside the sink and took off her shoes and socks. She watched me carefully as I eased off her clothes but she made no attempt to help. I felt pressed for time because the other children would be arriving in less than a half hour, and although they were used to washing and seeing others washed in the sink, I was afraid Sheila might feel too vulnerable at this point to have an audience. I asked her about it and she said she did not mind, but I still felt it would be better to finish before the others came.

She was a scrawny little whip of a child with all her ribs showing. I noticed the many scars on her body. "What happened here?" I asked as I washed one arm. A scar two inches long ran up the inside of it.

"That be where I brokeded my arm at, once."

"How'd you do that?"

"Falling down playing. The doctor putsa cast on it."

"You fell down playing?"

She nodded matter-of-factly, inspecting the scar. "I fall on the sidewalk. My Pa, he says I do be a godawful clumsy child. I hurt myself a lot."

In my mind was forming the question I had learned to ask of my kids; a question I dreaded. "Does your Pa ever do anything that leaves scars like these? Like spank you hard or something?" I asked.

She looked at me, her eyes clouding over. She regarded me so long in silence that I wished I had not asked. It was a personal question and perhaps I had not laid a firm enough foundation in our relationship to be so intimate. "My Pa, he wouldn't do that. He wouldn't hurt me bad. He loves me. He just hits me a little bit to make me good. You gotta do that to kids sometimes. But my Pa, he loves me. I just be a clumsy child to get so many scars." Her voice was tinged with defiance.

I nodded and lifted her out of the sink to dry her off. For several moments she did not speak to me. I had her on my lap and was drying her legs when she twisted around to look me in the eye. "You know what my Mama done though?"

"No."

"Here, I'll show you." She lifted the other leg up and pointed to a scar. "My Mama she take me out on the road and leave me there. She push me out of the car and I fall down so's a rock cutted up my leg right here. See." She fingered a white line. "My Pa, he loves me. He don't go leaving me on no roads. You ain't supposed to do that with little kids."

"No, you're not."

"My Mama, she don't love me so good."

In silence I began combing out her hair. I did not really want to hear any more because it hurt to listen to her; her voice was so calm and matter-of-fact that I felt that I shouldn't be listening to what she was saying. It was like reading someone's diary, the very calmness of the print making the words more pathetic.

"My Mama, she take Jimmie and go to California. That be where they live right now. Jimmie, he be my brother and he be four years old, 'cept that he only be two when my Mama, she leave. I ain't seen Jimmie in two whole years." She paused thoughtfully. "I miss Jimmie sort of. I wish I could see him again. He be a real nice boy." Again she turned around in my lap so she could see me. "You'd like Jimmie. He be a nice boy and don't yell

69

or be bad or anything. He be a nice boy to have in this here crazy kidses class. 'Cept I don't think he be crazy like me. You like Jimmie. My Mama do. She like Jimmie better'n me, that's why she tooked him and leaved me behind. You ought to have Jimmie in this here class. He don't do bad things like I do."

I hugged her to me. "Kitten, you're the one I'd want. Not Jimmie. He'll have his own teacher some day. I don't care what kids do, I just like them. That's all."

She sat back and looked at me, a bemused look falling across her face. "You do be a funny lady for a teacher. I think you be as crazy as us kidses be."

That fifth day, Friday, she still did not talk to the other kids although when asked a direct question she would answer any of the adults. At the end of the day after everyone had had ice cream and we had finished closing exercises, we were standing in line waiting for the buses to arrive to take the other children home. We had finished up a bit early and everyone was standing around in their snowsuits getting hot, so I suggested a song. Max shouted out that he wanted "If You're Happy and You Know It, Clap Your Hands," one of the few songs he would sing with the rest of us. It was a simple action song that required the children to clap, then stomp, then nod their heads. I looked over to see Sheila standing on the edge of the group not singing but paying close attention. When we had finished all the actions, the buses still had not arrived so I asked for suggestions for new actions. Tyler said, "If you're happy and you know it, jump up and down." So we sang a verse using Tyler's action. Again I asked for new actions. From her corner Sheila shyly raised her hand. With all our other problems and with so few children I just never got around to requesting that they do that unless we were having a moment of mass confusion. To see this little kid—who thus far had never spoken to the other children, who came in with a history of uncooperativeness—standing there with her hand up was a heart stopper.

"Sheila, do you have an idea?"

"Turn around?" she said diffidently.

And so we sang our song turning around. The first week had ended in the heat of success.

Sheila came alive in our room during the next weeks. She began speaking, first with reserve, and then with none. Sheila had thoughts on everything and was most articulate when given the chance. I was delighted to have a verbal child in the room. The other children enjoyed her company and I was tickled that she could tell me about so many things.

Sheila never brought up the burning incident, not during the early stages of our relationship, not later, not ever. Most of the more coherent kids in my class were aware of some of the reasons why they had been placed in there. We talked about those reasons regularly, during the times we set weekly and long-term goals for change, occasionally during morning topic and at other less formal times: out on the playground while we all stood shivering in the lee of the building too engrossed in conversation to go in, over lunch or art or cooking, alone together on the pillows in the secluded animal-cage corner. There seemed to be a pressing need in most of the kids to talk about these things.

The conversations were low-keyed and often casual, much experience having gone into my ability to discuss such topics as committing suicide or burning cats alive with the same casualness with which I made out my laundry list or asked about baseball scores. The kids did not need to knows the behaviors were wrong or that they frightened or repelled others—they already knew that. Otherwise they would not have been in my room in the first place. Instead they needed to explore the width and breadth and depth of those acts, how they felt when they did them, how they had expected they would feel and the seemingly meaningless myriad of details surrounding the episodes. Mostly I listened, asked a question or two if things were not clear, mmmm-hmmmed a lot to let them know I heard. And I kept us busy at dozens of mindless tasks like coloring or making papier mâché projects so that we could talk without having to look at one another, without having to acknowledge we were talking.

Sheila knew why she was there. From the second day on she continued to refer to us affectionately as a "crazy

71

class." And she was a crazy kid who did bad things. Often she would join the conversations. Yet not once was the abuse incident brought up. Not with the kids. Not with me or the other adults. Never. I did not suggest the topic either. Although I seldom avoided issues, this one I felt instinctively I should leave alone, for no other reason than what my gut told me. So we never discussed it. I never found out what had been going through Sheila's mind that cold November evening.

I remained perplexed about her speech patterns. The more she talked, the more obvious the discrepancy was between the way Sheila spoke and the way the rest of us did. There were no reports of her father speaking any sort of dialect. He was a native of the area and should have spoken in the same manner as the rest of us. The major variations were word insertions, especially "do" and "be," and the absence of a past tense. The word "do" was used as an auxiliary verb, inserted at will throughout Sheila's conversations. "Be" took the place of "am," "is" and "are." For Sheila, the past tense simply did not exist with very few exceptions. Everything was spoken as if it were in the present or future. This mystified me because she had a good command of very difficult tenses such as conditionals like "should" and "would," and was capable of putting together complex sentences far beyond the grasp of most six-year-olds. Repeatedly, I taped samples of her speech and sent them off to experts to be analyzed. In the meantime, I let her speak as she chose.

Allan, the school psychologist, gave Sheila an IQ and reading test. The IQ test Sheila topped out, earning the highest possible score. Allan was astonished, coming out of his little room shaking his head. He had never had a child do that on the test he was using, and certainly had never expected it from a child they would place in a class like mine. Sheila read and comprehended on a fifth grade level, despite the fact that no one had ever taught her to read. Allan left that day, vowing to find a test that could measure her IQ.

Each morning before school Sheila and I worked on hygiene. I bought a plastic bucket at the discount store and put a comb, brush, washcloth, towel, soap, lotion and

72

toothbrush in it. Most days Sheila was willing to wash and brush her teeth, if I would fix her hair. She delighted in the hair clips. I bought another package like the kind that I wore and Sheila guarded them all like a king's treasure. Each morning she went through them, counting them and deciding which ones she would wear. Each evening she took them out of her hair, laying them carefully in the folds of the towel. Again she counted them to make sure no one had taken any. Her clothes were a bit more of a problem. I kept clean underpants at school and insisted she change every morning. We never discussed the problem because I deduced that after the first day, it was a sensitive area. I did, however, make sure she changed, regardless of what subjects we mentioned. On Mondays Whitney trotted Sheila's overalls and shirt down to the Laundromat around the corner from the school. It was hardly a foolproof solution but at least Sheila did not stink so much anymore. All in all, she was a handsome child cleaned up. She had thick, long blond hair and much to the pleasure of all of us she had sparkly eyes and a ready smile that showed three gaps on the bottom awaiting new teeth.

To my relief one problem which I had anticipated but which never materialized was Sheila's bus ride to and from the migrant camp. With such a terrible history of uncontrollable behavior, Sheila, unsupervised on a bus, was something I could not imagine working out well. However, my fears proved to be unfounded. Perhaps putting her with forty high school students was enough to intimidate even Sheila.

Anton or I walked her to and from the bus, but once on it, she settled down in a seat toward the back. The only incident that ever occurred was in late January after she had been on the route for some time. We had walked her to the bus in the evening and put her on. However, by the time the bus had arrived at the migrant camp and the high school students had climbed off, Sheila was not there. The bus driver stood up from his seat and looked back, but the bus was empty. Alarmed because the bus only made two stops before the camp and he had not seen her disembark at either of them, the driver called me at home to make sure she had gotten on. I told him she had. There were more than a few panicky moments before the bus driver called back. Apparently, Sheila had gotten down on the floor by the rear tire where the heat came in and she fell asleep. After she discovered that warm, vibrating spot, she regularly curled up on the floor under the seat and slept during the hour ride both in and out. The driver always checked after that, to make sure she awakened and got off. The high school students, at first only tolerant of her presence, began to save that seat near the heater for her, began also to give her book bags or extra sweaters for a pillow and to see she was walked home on those nights she was too sleepy to be reliable.

A problem that was not solving itself was Sheila's father. I had tried relentlessly to get hold of him for a conference. He had no phone so I sent a note home with Sheila asking him to come to school. No response. I sent a second note. Again no response. I sent a third note saying I was coming to visit him at his home. When the evening came that Anton and I went out, the house was empty. I was getting the distinct impression he did not want to see me. Finally I contacted Sheila's social worker. Together we went out only to be greeted at the door by Sheila. Her father was gone.

I wanted to see him very badly. First I wanted to make some arrangements for Sheila to get proper clothing. I had mentioned this to the social worker. Although Sheila had only one outfit, my main concern was her outerwear. She owned only a boy's thin cotton jacket, something like a baseball Windbreaker. She had no gloves, no hat, no boots. And it was, after all, January. The temperature hovered around 20 degrees most days and had even been below zero on occasion. Sheila would arrive at school almost blue some mornings after her walk from the high school two blocks away. In desperation I had taken my car to get her on the worst days. I gave her more to wear at recess, but the one time I sent things home, they came back the next day in a paper bag. Sheila remarked with embarrassment that she had gotten a spanking for accepting "charity." The social worker explained that they had repeatedly gotten on the father for this and had even taken him downtown once to buy clothes for Sheila from his welfare check. But apparently he had returned the clothes later. You couldn't force the

74

man, she said, shrugging. She did not want to endanger Sheila by forcing the issue because it was a known fact that he took his anger out on the child. Wasn't that child abuse? I had asked. Not technically. There were not any marks on her. I had slammed the door in frustration after the social worker left. Not any marks on her, huh? Then what the hell was she doing in my class? If that wasn't a mark, I didn't know what was.

During the hours that school was in session, I tried to provide her with all the experiences that her disturbance or circumstances had robbed her of. She came alive. Every moment of her day was filled with exploring and chattering. The first weeks she followed me around all day long. Everywhere I went, when I turned around there she would be, clutching a book to her chest or a box of math cubes. A silly smile would spill over her lips when she caught my eye, and she'd scuttle up ready to share. I had to divide my time equally with the other children, of course, but this did not deter her. She would stand patiently behind me waiting until I had finished. Sometimes I would feel a hand tentatively take hold of my belt as she got braver and longed for more physical contact. Anton would laugh and kid me in the teacher's lounge about looking like a subway, because as I walked around the room helping the other children, Sheila would go with me, one hand locked into my belt like a seasoned straphanger.

During those first weeks of intense devotion, I was both thankful and dismayed for the two hours we had alone after school. My planning time was shot. Much to Chad's displeasure I was having to haul my work home and do it in the evenings. Anton groused about never getting to talk over matters anymore unless we both came in at seven thirty in the morning. But for Sheila it was ideal. She needed undivided attention.

For all of her six years she had been unwanted, ignored, rejected. Pushed out of cars, pushed out of people's lives. Now there was someone to hold her and talk to her and cuddle her. Sheila soaked up every little bit of intimacy I could spare. Despite the inconvenience of losing those two hours of planning time, I felt less anxious about dragging her around all day hanging on my belt and ignoring her while I worked with the other children, because after school she had me all to herself.

75

The other children were as delighted as Anton and I were to see Sheila blossom. Notes filled the Kobold's Box scribbled in childish hand. Most of the children were relieved that she did not smell so often or so badly and were quick to comment on that. But they also perceived her budding attempts at kindness.

Sheila had evidently not had much of an opportunity to learn how to be considerate of others or how to be kind. She had been busy surviving and altruism had little place in survival. Consequently, she was used to having to fight for what she wanted. When someone got the place in line she had chosen, she socked that person hard enough to win it back. If another child had a toy she wanted, she grabbed it, wrestled it out of the child's hands and scuttled off to safety with it to hiss angrily at anyone who tried to take it away. In many ways she was much cruder and more obnoxious in her directness than even Peter, but hers was an animal-like aggressiveness, without malice.

I knew that, after six years, it was not going to be a simple matter to convince her that there was another way to do things. My reprimands and cautions and forced marches to the quiet corner did not noticeably dent her behavior. But the Kobold's Box did.

Each night Sheila listened carefully as I read the notes and complimented the children who earned them. Greedily she would count hers after each session and, if given the opportunity, she would count other children's also to see if they got more or less than she did. I tried to discourage that activity. The other kids were not competitive and did not feel the need to measure their worth by the number of notes they received. I did not want them to start. But Sheila could not resist. Her meager portion of self-confidence would not let her rest. Over and over again she wanted to prove that she was the best child in the class, the smartest, the hardest-working, my favorite. When I steadfastly refused to confirm that, she set out to prove it to herself with notes in the Kobold's Box. But that eluded her. She could show me how well she read. That was simple; it only entailed getting out a book. She could show me how well she did math. That, too, was simple. But she could not figure out how to be kind or polite or considerate in order to earn herself more notes.

One afternoon after school she had stayed by the table

where I was taking apart a science experiment. "How come Tyler gets so many notes?" she asked. "She gets more than anybody else does. Do you give them to her?"

"No, you know that. Everybody writes out notes."

"How come she gets more?" She cocked her head. "What she do? How come everybody likes her so good?"

"Well," I considered the matter a moment. "For one thing, she's polite. When she wants something she asks, and almost always says please. And thank you too. That makes a person feel more like helping her or being with her, because she makes you feel good for it."

Sheila frowned, looking down at her hands. After a long pause she looked accusingly at me. "How come you never tell me you want me to say please and thank you? I don't know you want that. How come you tell Tyler and you don't tell me?"

I looked at her in disbelief. "I didn't tell Tyler, Sheila. It's just something people do. Everybody likes other people to be polite."

"I don't know that. Nobody ever told me," she said reproachfully. "I never know you want me to do that."

In considering the matter, I knew she was right. I probably never had told her. It was one of those things I took for granted a child would know, especially a bright child like her. I had just assumed she knew. But the unfairness of the assumption was dawning on me. Sheila might never had heard those words in her environment. Or perhaps they had never been meaningful to her before.

"I'm sorry, Sheil. I thought you knew."

"I don't. I can say them if I know you want me to."

I nodded. "I do. They're good words to use, because they make other people feel good. That's important. People like you better for it."

"Will they tell me I'm a nice girl?"

"It'll help them see that you are."

And so, little by little she began to attend to what others were doing to be kind and considerate. When she did not understand, she asked. At other times when it occurred to me that she did not know, I would tell her during one of our quiet moments.

CHAPTER 8

UNFORTUNATELY, AS IN ALL GARDENS OF Eden, there were a few snakes. During that first month there were two problems that we did not seem able to lick.

The first problem was perhaps not as major as it felt. Despite all her progress, Sheila steadfastly refused to do paperwork. The instant a piece of paper was given to her, she destroyed it. Occasionally under dire threat from Anton or me, she would not tear it up immediately but actually appear to be working on it. However, it never reached the correction basket. Partway through she would rip it to shreds or scribble over it or crumple it into a tight little wad, stuffing it under the radiator or into the rabbit's cage to be eaten.

I tried any number of methods to stop her. I taped the work to the table so that she could not get it up. Then she simply scribbled over it until it tore. I put it into plastic folders. She would sit before it and refuse to pick up her crayon. On one occasion, she even ate the crayon. I tried using workbooks. But they were more expensive and I got angrier when they were ruined in one sitting. I tried Mrs. Barthuly's technique of laminating, since we had no air conditioner. It was a costly, time-consuming alternative and when presented with one, Sheila would just sit, refusing to do anything. I put the work on the chalkboard. She would erase it when I wasn't looking. There was not a method I could think of that she could not foil.

Sheila was not selective. If it required a written answer, she would not touch it. This included all the academics, coloring sheets and even art projects. She had no objection to oral work or even letting Anton or Whitney or me fill out a paper for her. But she would not do it herself.

Needless to say, this caused considerable friction between us. I tried all my tricks. I sent her to the quiet corner. But she would sit motionless and soundless for such a long time that I felt that was not solving the problem. I did not want her to miss too much of the program simply sitting in a chair. Unlike the first week when the quiet corner provided a means of getting control of her behavior, this did not. The quiet corner was not intended as punishment. So I was not concerned when the children sat there crying or struggling. They were out of control and trying to regain it. But when the child simply went there and sat, it became punishment. Occasionally a few minutes of punishment were warranted, but not long stretches at a time. So if I sent her to the corner and she went and was still not willing to do paperwork after twenty minutes of sitting, I let it drop. My winning the power struggle was not so important as keeping her active and participating in class. Moreover, I was concerned that something else lay behind her refusal to do paperwork. Unless she were angry, there was little else Sheila refused to do outrightly. We had long ago settled who was boss in the classroom and I did not feel she was testing. She went to ridiculous heights to please me in other ways, so it did not make sense to me that she was holding out on this one thing simply to irk me.

But admittedly the behavior did. And not just a little. I became obsessed with it after the third week, storming into the teachers' lounge and raging at the other teachers after school. At night Chad bore the brunt of my frustrations. Finally, one day, in desperation, I dittoed one worksheet off on a whole ream of paper. I maneuvered Sheila over to a table and sat her down at math. I decided that if we had to sit there until Valentine's Day and go through all 500 copies, we would.

"We're going to do this math worksheet today, Sheila. All I want is this one sheet and it's got easy problems on it."

She looked at me distrustfully. "I don't wanna do that."

"Well, it isn't your choice today." I tapped the paper on the table agitatedly with one finger. "Come on, let's get started."

She sat staring at me. I could tell she was leery of the situation. I had never forced her in such a direct confrontation and she did not seem to be able to tell what to expect from me. Inside myself my own irritation was clenching my organs. My stomach was tight and knotted, my heart beating rapidly. For a split second I wanted to retreat, but my anger over all these weeks of refusal overwhelmed me.

"Do it." I could hear my voice louder and sharper in my ears than I wanted it to be. I reached over and grabbed a pencil, shoving it into her hand. "I said do the paper. Now do it, Sheila."

She wadded up the first paper. I carefully straightened it out and taped it down to the table. Sheila gouged it out with the pencil. Grimly we struggled, me putting out new copies, Sheila ripping at them. Math period passed and the litter of destroyed dittos deepened around our chairs. The others rose for freetime. Sheila glanced around in concern. Freetime was her favorite period and already she noticed Tyler was getting out the little toy people she liked to play with.

"Finish this paper and you can go," I stated, taping a new one down. I had swallowed my anger but a subdued sort of frenzy remained, causing my pulse to continue to run faster.

Sheila was losing patience with me. Angry little grunts were coming out with her heavy breaths. We went through another half-dozen copies of the worksheet. Moving my chair close to hers I pinned her in her chair against the table. Then I taped down a new sheet. Holding down her free hand, I took her other in mine. "I'll help you, Sheila, if you can't do it by yourself," I said doggedly. I could feel perspiration soaking my shirt.

80

Sheila began to scream, cutting loose with an earsplitting yell. Thankfully she was left-handed as I was, so I could move her hand. I asked her the answer to the first problem. At first she refused to say but then angrily shouted it out. I pushed her hand along the paper, writing a 3. Sheila struggled violently, trying to knock loose my hold of her chair, trying to bite me. Second problem now. Again I dragged the answer out of her and forced her to write it.

We struggled the rest of freetime and finished the paper with her screaming protests and me forcing her hand. The second I let go, she scrabbled the paper up from the tape and shredded it before I could catch her hands. Angrily she threw the paper in my face and broke away from my hold, knocking over the chair. Running to the other side of the classroom she turned to glower at me.

"I HATE YOU!" she screamed as loudly as possible. The other children were finishing their snacks and getting ready for recess, but they paused, watching us. "I hate you! I hate you! I hate you!" Then her frustration with me overpowered her and she stood shrieking wordlessly from her corner behind the animal cages.

Anton cleared the other kids out to recess, but I remained sitting at the table. Expecting her to go off into one of her destructive rages, I was poised to catch her. But she didn't. After a few moments she regained her composure and stopped screaming. However, she remained across the room, staring at me reproachfully. She seemed on the verge of tears, her mouth turned down, her chin quivering. I was beginning to feel like a first-class heel. Her disappointment in me for behaving so antagonistically was bright in her eyes. As I watched her, I knew I had done the wrong thing. I had been desperate, my teacher's instinct to get work accomplished on paper having overcome my better sense. But I shouldn't have let that happen. It had been wrong. I hated myself for allowing such an unimportant thing rule me.

I regarded her. Bad feelings rippled through me, recriminations, self-doubt. Had I destroyed our relationship? We had been doing so well in the three weeks since she had come. Had I screwed it all up in one morning? She watched me. For long, eternal moments we looked at each other in silence.

Slowly Sheila came toward me. Her eyes were still on me all the time, big, wary, accusing eyes. She came over to the far edge of the table. Tracing an invisible design on the smooth top, she studied it before looking back up at me. "You not be very nice to me." Her voice was heavy with feeling.

"No, I guess I wasn't, was I?" I felt the silence again. "I'm sorry, Sheila. I shouldn't have done that."

"You shouldn't oughta be mean to me. I be one of your kids."

"I'm sorry. I just got upset because you never do papers. I just wanted you to do papers like everyone else does. It makes me mad that you won't ever do them because it is important to me that you do. I got angry."

She studied me carefully. Her lower lip was shoved out and her eyes were hurt-looking, but she sidled closer. "Do you still like me?"

"Of course I still like you."

"But you be mad at me and yell."

"Sometimes people get mad. Even at people they like a lot. It doesn't mean they stop liking them. They're just mad. And after a while the anger goes away and they still like each other. I like you as much as ever."

She pressed her lips together. "I don't really hate you."

"I know that. You were just angry like I was."

"You yell at me. I don't like you to yell at me like that. It hurts my ears."

"Look, kitten, I was wrong. I'm sorry. But I can't make it not happen because it already did. I'm sorry. For right now we won't worry about paperwork. We'll do it some other time when you feel like it."

"I ain't never going to feel like it."

My shoulders sagged with discouragement. "Well, then maybe we'll never do any."

She looked at me quizzically. "There gotta be paperwork."

I sighed tiredly. "Not really, I suppose. There are things more important. Besides, maybe someday you will feel like it. We'll do it then."

And so I gave up the paperwork war. Or at least the battle.

I can never understand what it is about being human that allows one to become fixed on small matters and

82

think the world will collapse if things don't go just the way one wants them. Once I got that struggle out of my system, I could never understand why it had been so important to me. But for those first few weeks, it had.

The second problem Sheila presented was much more serious and much less easily resolved. She had a keenly developed sense of revenge that knew no limits. When crossed or taken advantage of, Sheila retaliated with devastating force. Her intelligence made it all the more frightening because she could perceive quickly what was valuable to a person and that was what she abused to get back for being wronged. When Sarah kicked snow on her at recess, Sheila systematically destroyed all of Sarah's artwork around the room. For art-loving Sarah this was crushing. Anton got angry with Sheila running in the halls to lunch one day and she returned afterwards and throttled all the baby gerbils Anton had brought to school that morning on loan from his son. Her cold, clear-eyed appraisal of everyone's sensitivities left me chilled.

But it went beyond destroying papers or even baby gerbils. It was calculated and long-abiding, and often over events which were not intentional. Sheila had to be watched every second. Even when we did think we were watching her carefully, she managed to get away from us.

Lunch hour was the most dangerous time of day. Neither Anton nor I wanted to give up our only break to police Sheila constantly. The lunch aides were clearly still frightened of her, although they did supervise her once more.

One day while Anton and I were in the teachers' lounge finishing up our sandwiches, one of the aides came shrieking in to us, Sheila's name spilling out incoherently. Having nightmares of a repeat of the first day, we dashed out after her as she left.

Sheila had gotten into one of the other teachers' rooms. In a short period of time, only ten or fifteen minutes, she destroyed the room completely. All the student desks were awry or knocked over, personal belongings strewn about. The window blinds were pulled down, books were out of the bookcase, the screen of one of the teaching machines was shattered. I could not have dreamed of further destruction in such a short time.

I yanked open the door. "Sheila!" She whirled around, her eyes dark and forbidding. A pointer was clutched in one hand. "Drop that!"

She stared at me for a long moment but let the pointer drop. She had been with us three weeks. By now she knew when I meant business. If I could get her to drop what she was doing and come over to me, I could take her out calmly. I knew better than to spook her so that she would flee. She would do more damage if she bolted and would become so frightened that she could not be reasoned with. She already had that wild-animal, frenzied look in her eye and I realized how tenuous her hold on control was.

However, as I looked around the room at the disaster, I could not imagine what we were going to do. I was flooded with discouragement at the fact that she would do this kind of thing, that I had let it happen. Sitting in the quiet corner hardly seemed adequate to cover hundreds of dollars' damage. This was also not my room. It was somebody else's. So I knew the matter was out of my hands.

By the time I had coaxed Sheila over to the door, Mr. Collins and the teacher, Mrs. Holmes, whose room this was, were behind me. When I finally got hold of Sheila's hand, Mr. Collins began to roar.

I suppose he roared with very good reason. But I knew what his solution to the problem was going to include. Mr. Collins was of the old school where most infractions were cured, or at least helped, by the paddle. He took hold of Sheila's arm. I already had her by the overall strap and did not let go.

We eyed each other, neither of us speaking. Sheila was stretched out between us.

I could not let him take her. Not after all this time of reassuring her that she could never be hurt here. There had been too many spankings in her past already. And too many people who had broken their promises. I could not let this happen.

Still the principal and I did not speak. However, that did not diminish the strength of the challenge. Under my fingers on her shoulder, I could feel the tenseness of Sheila's muscles.

When he finally did speak, Mr. Collins' voice came out in a hoarse whisper pushed between gritted teeth. He made it clear that not only was Sheila going down to the office for a paddling but I was coming along as witness.

Oh cripes, I was thinking. All I wanted to do was argue with him while Sheila was strung out between us, like two dogs fighting over a bone. But there wasn't much choice. I could not agree with him. Certainly I did not want Sheila to think I did.

We were hissing back and forth, one- or two-word responses mostly. He was losing patience with me.

"So help me God, Miss Hayden, you come with me right now or you're not going to have a job by the time this day is out. I don't care what I have to do. Is that clear?"

I stared at him. All sorts of things came into my head then. I had tenure. I belonged to the union. He had no power to fire me. Those things all came to me, but on a very academic level. What came at gut level was fear. What would happen to me if I got fired? Could I ever find another teaching job in town? Who would take care of my class? I had a history of rash and impulsive actions. Was this going to be one more? And what for? A kid bound for the state hospital? Here I was about to lose my job over a kid I'd barely known three weeks, who sooner or later would be elsewhere anyway, and who by all accounts wasn't very important to anybody anyhow. What would everyone think if I lost my job? Would Chad still want me? How would I explain it to my mom? What would people think? For the worst excuse of all, I let go of that overall strap.

Mr. Collins turned and took Sheila down the hall. I followed at a distance and felt like Benedict Arnold. Yet maybe they were right. I had lost control in a major way twice in three weeks with this kid. Maybe she did need a state hospital placement. I did not know. This had gotten to be more than I could manage.

I flopped into a chair in Mr. Collins' office. Sheila was calm. Far calmer than I. She came in beside Mr. Collins and stood complacently, not looking at me and not making any sound. Mr. Collins shut the door. From his desk drawer he took out a long paddle. Sheila did not flinch as he sized it up next to her.

I was bitter. Why did he have to have such neolithic methods of education? What kind of man was he? A lusty, full-bodied hate rose in me. How could he do this to me? How could I let him? After all my reassurances to her that I did not whip kids, what would she think of me now? What would I think of myself, now that I knew when the going got rough I would opt for my own skin?

Through the chaos in my own head, I was suddenly and deeply touched by Sheila's innocent courage. She glanced at me briefly and then looked back at Mr. Collins. She looked very much like any other six-year-old just then. Her lips were parted to reveal the gaps where teeth had fallen out. Her eyes were wide and round, the fear in them disguised enough so that if one had not known her, one would not have recognized it for what it was. I saw the little white and orange duck barrettes in her hair and thought how much she liked them. Those were her favorites, her lucky clips, she told me one day. *Well, your luck's run out this time, kid,* I thought. Like so many other times before. The duck clips seemed obscene in this place.

She stood so staunchly; no six-year-old should be able to do that. I wondered how often a board had been shown to her. Yet about her persisted such a little child's innocence; the duck barrettes, the long, impossibly straight hair not quite captured in pigtails, the worn overalls. I felt like crying. But the tears would be for myself for finding out I did not have the kind of strength that she had.

My viscera crinkled. This should not be happening.

But it was. Mr. Collins stated flatly that he had had it. Did she know what she had done? No response. She might even be suspended from school, he said. I knew the lecture was as much for my benefit as Sheila's. We were both being put in our places. He told her she was getting three whacks of the board. She had sucked her lips between her teeth. She watched him without blinking.

"Lean over and grab your ankles."

She stared without moving.

"Lean over and take hold of your ankles, Sheila."

She did not move.

"If I have to tell you one more time, I'll add another whack. Now bend over."

"Sheila, please," I said. "Please do as he says."

Still no response. Her eyes flickered toward mine a moment.

Mr. Collins yanked her down roughly and with a whoosh the board hit her. She fell on her knees on that first whack, but her face remained unchanged. Mr. Collins lifted her back to her feet. Again came the whack. Again she fell to her knees. The last two whacks she stood up and did not fall. But not a sound came out of her, not a tear came to her eyes. I could tell this had infuriated Mr. Collins.

I sat watching, numbed. After all my reassurance to her, it had come to this. I had worked so hard, so damned hard on this kid. I normally never let myself fully realize how much I invested in the children. Like the little fears and discouragements that I kept shooing out of consciousness during day-to-day living, I also spooked away into hiding how much the kids really meant to me. Because I knew that if I was aware, I would feel even more disheartened when my kids failed. Or when I did. That was what burned so many people out in this business: knowing they cared too much. So I tried not to see it. I was a dreamer. But my dream was a very expensive one. For all of us.

Mr. Collins had me sign a witness form that I had been present when he had paddled her. Then wearily I took Sheila's hand and we went down the hall.

I did not know what to do next. My head was spinning. When I got to the classroom door, I peered through the window. Anton had started afternoon activities and Whitney was there. Things seemed peaceful enough. I looked down at Sheila. "We need to talk, kiddo."

Knocking on the door, I waited for Anton to answer. When he arrived, I explained that I wanted to be alone with Sheila a little while, that too much had happened and I needed to get some things straightened out. I asked if he thought he and Whitney could manage while we were gone. He nodded with a smile. So I left them, one uneducated migrant worker and a fourteen-year-old kid, in charge of eight crazy children. The ludicrousness of the situation struck me and I almost laughed. But I could find no laughter in me just then.

I ended up taking Sheila into a book closet because I could not find anywhere else we could be alone undisturbed. I hauled in two teensy chairs, turned on the light and sat down, shutting the door behind me. For a long moment we stared at each other.

"Why on earth do you do those things?" I asked, my discouragement ringing clearly in my voice.

"You ain't gonna make me talk."

"Oh geez, Sheila, come off it. I can't play games with you. Now don't do that to me." I could not tell if she were angry or what. Inwardly, I wanted to apologize to her for having given in and letting Mr. Collins take her. But I did not do it. The need was more mine. I wanted to be forgiven.

We regarded each other without talking and the silence seemed to draw into eternity. Finally I shook my head and sighed wearily. "Look, that whole thing didn't turn out so well. I'm sorry."

Still silence. She would not talk to me. Her gaze was unwavering and I had to look away. Outside the door of the book closet I could hear classes getting ready for recess, noisy and rambunctious, such that they thudded against the door. Inside it was so quiet no one would ever know we were in there.

I looked at her. Looked away. Looked back. She stared. "Good God, Sheila, what *is* it you want out of me?"

The pupils in her eyes dilated. "Are you mad at me?"

"You could say that, yes. I'm just a little mad at everybody right now."

"You gonna whip me?"

My shoulders sagged. "No, I'm not. Like I told you a million times now, I don't whip kids."

"Why not?"

I looked at her in dismal disbelief. "Why should I? It doesn't help any, does it?"

"It helps me."

"Does it? Does it really, Sheila? Did what Mr. Collins just do to you help you?"

"My Pa," she said softly, "he says it be the only way to make me decent. He whips me and I must be betterer, 'cause he ain't never leaved me on no highway like my Mama done."

My heart melted. I certainly hadn't intended it to. I had been so angry at her for all this trouble she had caused. But my heart melted when she spoke. Jesus, I thought, what did this kid expect out of people. I reached an arm out to her. "Come here, Sheil, and let me hold you."

Willingly she came, climbing up into my lap clumsily like a toddler. She wrapped her arms around my ribs and clutched me tightly. I pressed her close. I was doing it as much for myself as I was for her because I didn't know what to do. God Almighty, I hurt inside.

What were we going to do? She had to stop this destructiveness, that went without saying. But how? What were a bunch of tipped-over desks and broken window shades against a little girl? Even if she had done a million dollars' worth of damage, what was that against a life? If they sent her out of the school, suspended her, she wouldn't come back. I had been in the business long enough to know that. Sooner or later, it would be off to the state hospital as planned. What then? What chance did a six-year-old have of coming out of a state hospital to live a normal life? I doubted it had ever happened. We'd lose her, without most of us even realizing she had been there at all. This bright, creative little girl who had never had a chance at life, would never get one. Were a bunch of lousy desks worth that much?

"What're we gonna do, Sheila?" I asked, rocking her in my arms. "You just can't keep doing these sorts of things and I don't know how to stop you."

"I won't do it again."

"I wish you wouldn't. But let's not make any promises we can't keep just now, okay? I just want you to tell me why you did it to begin with. I want to understand that."

"I dunno. I do be awful mad at her. She yell at me at lunch and it not be my fault. It be Susannah's fault but she yell at me. I be mad." Her voice quivered. "Do they gonna make me go away?"

"I don't know, honey."

"I don't want them to." Her voice rose suddenly to a little squeak, betraying her nearness to tears. "I won't never ever do that again. I wanna stay. I wanna stay in this here school. I won't never do it again, I promise." She pressed her face against me.

I stroked her hair, feeling the duck clips under my fingers. "Sheila," I asked, "I never see you cry. Don't you ever feel like it?"

"I don't never cry."

"Why not?"

"Ain't nobody can hurt me that ways."

I looked down at her. The cold perception in her statement was fearsome. "What do you mean?"

"Ain't nobody can hurt me. They don't know I hurt if I don't cry. So they can't hurt me. Ain't nobody can make me cry neither. Not even my Pa when he whips me. Not even Mr. Collins. You seen that. I don't cry even when he hits me with the stick. You seen that, didn't you?"

"Yes, I saw it. But don't you want to cry? Didn't it hurt?"

For a very long moment she did not respond. She took hold of one of my hands in both of hers. "It sort of hurts." She looked up, her eyes unreadable. "Sometimes I do cry a little, at night sometimes. My Pa, he don't come home 'til it be real late sometimes and I have to be by myself and I get scared. Sometimes I cry a little bit; it get wet right here on my eyes. But I make it go away. Crying don't do no good, and it makes me think of Jimmie and my Mama if I cry. It makes me miss them."

"Sometimes it does help."

"It don't never help me. I ain't never gonna cry. Never."

She had turned around so that she straddled my legs and was facing me. I had my arms around her back. She fingered my shirt buttons while she talked.

"Do you ever cry?" she asked.

I nodded. "Sometimes. Mostly when I feel bad, I cry. I can't help it much, I just do. But it makes me feel better. Crying is a good thing in a way. It washes out the hurt, if you give it a chance."

She shrugged. "I don't do it."

"Sheil, what're we gonna do to fix up what you did in Mrs. Holmes' room?"

Again she shrugged. She feigned involvement in twisting one of my buttons.

"I want your ideas. I'm not going to whip you and I

don't think suspending you is a good idea either. But we've got to do something. I want your ideas."

"You could make me sit in the quiet corner the rest of the day and you could take away the housekeeping corner for a week or something. You could take away the dolls from me."

"I don't want to punish you. Mr. Collins did that already. I want a way to make it better for Mrs. Holmes. I want to fix up what happened in there."

A pause ensued. "Maybe I could pick it up."

"I think that's a good idea. But what about being sorry? Could you apologize?"

She tugged at the button. "I don't know."

"Are you sorry?"

She nodded slowly. "I be sorry this here happened."

"Apologizing is a good thing to learn to do. It makes people feel better about you. Shall we practice together saying you're sorry and offering to pick up, so it'll be easier to do? I can be Mrs. Holmes and we'll practice."

Sheila fell against me heavily, pressing her face into my breasts. "I just want you to hold me for a little bit first. My butt do be fierce sore and I wanna wait 'til it feels better. I don't wanna think now."

With a smile I clutched her to me and we sat together in the dim light of the book closet, waiting—she for relief for her bottom and the courage for what lay ahead; I for the world to change.

CHAPTER 9

Resolving that situation did not turn out to be simple. Sheila and I did go to Mrs. Holmes' room and Sheila apologized and offered to pick up. As I had hoped, Sheila's childlike innocence, her small size, her natural beauty all brought out the motherliness in Mrs. Holmes. She was willing to accept Sheila's attempts to make amends.

On the other hand, it was not so easy with Mr. Collins. This had been the last straw for him, not only for Sheila, but for my class. Everything came to a head—including things not even related to Sheila's destructiveness. The two of us simply had different value systems, each of which seemed better in our own eyes. It all came out in a full-scale war after Sheila's incident and finally Ed Somers had to come and mediate. In no uncertain terms Mr. Collins wanted Sheila out of the school. The child was violent, uncontrolled, dangerous and destructive. She frightened the other children with her behavior, as well as the other teachers and the staff. She had caused $700 worth of damage in Mrs. Holmes' room alone. There was a point, he said, when society had the right to protect itself from harm. An identified threat such as this child should not be allowed to run loose in a public school. She belonged in the state hospital. Why wasn't she there?

I tried to explain Sheila's progress in my room. I explained how it had only taken three days to crack through this child and get her to work productively in the classroom. I spoke of her IQ, of her history of abuse and abandonment. I implored Ed to let me keep her. This was just one incident, I said. I'd watch her better after this. I'd give up my own lunch hour if I had to. But give me another chance, I asked. Let me try again. I wouldn't be so careless.

The mood was grim. Ed explained to me that they had the very real pressure from parents to consider. When word got out from the children in Mrs. Holmes' class, parents would call. And the court had arranged for her commitment before I had ever entered the picture. My room was the holding tank. I shouldn't get so involved, Ed said politely, but firmly. It was affecting my better judgment. He smiled sadly. It was nice she was making progress, but that was not why she had been placed with me. She was there to wait until a space came open at the hospital. That was all.

As I listened to him I could feel the lump in my throat and the stinging in my eyes. I did not want to cry in front of them. I did not want them to know they were getting to me that much. But I could feel the tears starting. My rational side kept urging calmness. They were not being intentionally cruel; indeed, they probably were not being cruel at all. But it felt that way to me. Goddamn them, what were they doing to me? I was a teacher. My job was to teach. I wasn't a jailer. Or was that all Ed had wanted when he had established my class? I was full of recriminations. What had they thought they had given me but a little girl—a scared, hurt, mistreated six-year-old. What was it that was so frightening about her? Now they told me that I didn't have to worry about her; she was only with me to wait. She could have sat in that chair of hers for however many months it took for the space in the state hospital to come through, and then she could leave. I had obviously misunderstood the matter. I had thought I was supposed to be her teacher.

Ed leaned forward resting his elbows on the table and blowing into his hands. He tried to reassure me, telling me not to get upset. He was embarrassed that the situation was making me cry and for a moment I was pleased he was. I wanted everyone as unhappy as I. But the moment passed and the gloom settled over all of us.

I left the room still tearful, went directly to my car and drove home. Feeling bitter and resentful, I feared I would need more than "Star Trek" to calm me that evening. My idealism had taken a mighty blow. I had learned some people were not even worth $700.

As always, Chad proved the calm center in my storm. Listening to me rage, he shook his head good-naturedly. Go to bed, he advised, it wasn't so bad as it seemed. Despite my feelings, it wasn't me against the world. It'd come out in the end, everything always does. Not in a mood to be placated, I shut myself in the bathroom and sobbed through a forty-five-minute shower. Chad was still sitting in the living room pulling a string for the cat when I emerged. Chad smiled. And then I smiled. I wasn't happy, but I was resigned.

It did not turn out so badly as I had anticipated. An education had to be provided for every child and I was at that moment Sheila's only source of education. In compromise, Ed told Mr. Collins that he could have an extra lunch aide solely to supervise my room and that Sheila was never under any circumstances to leave my room except under my direct supervision. The matter was at least temporarily settled.

Despite the furor over Sheila's placement, things were going smoothly in class. We were becoming a group again, adjusting to Sheila's being with us. February had dawned cold and crisp with a groundhog's promise of six more weeks of winter. Sheila was fitting in and we were quite happily twelve. I appreciated those unexpected days of peace because they were rare in our class.

Academically, Sheila was plunging ahead. I could hardly find enough to keep her agile mind busy. I had dropped the paperwork altogether, conceding her the victory, although I had to admit still thinking about it. Whitney, Anton and I tested her orally and had discussions with her over what she was doing. She was an avid reader, consuming books faster than I could find them. I was thankful for this new interest because without the paperwork, which makes up a good share of each child's academic day, she finished her assignments rapidly.

Socially Sheila was making slower progress, but it was steady. She and Sarah had become friends and were beginning to share the typical pleasures of small girls' friendships. I also assigned Sheila to help Susannah Joy to learn her colors. This had a multiple effect: it gave me a much-needed helper; it occupied Sheila's extra time; it gave her responsibility; and it helped Sheila learn the finer points of an interpersonal relationship. An added benefit was the boost to Sheila's self-confidence. She was elated to be on the giving end for once and have someone need her. Some evenings after school she would busily make materials and carry on long earnest discussions with Anton or me about things she could do with Susannah to help Susie learn. Watching her, I always wanted to laugh, wondering if I looked like that to someone watching me. But she took the job with such innocent seriousness that I contained myself.

Sheila was beginning to grow away from needing to follow me around all day long. She still watched me often and would sit nearby if given a choice, but she did not need physical contact all the time. On bad days when things had gone wrong before she came to school, or when the other kids gave her a hard time, or even when I reprimanded her, it was not unusual to feel her hand go through my belt and for a while once more, she would move around the room with me while I worked. I did not discourage it; I felt she needed the security of knowing I was not going to leave her. The line was fine between dependence and overdependence, but I had noticed that most of my kids went through a period of intense involvement and attachment in the beginning. It seemed to be a natural phase and if things progressed right, the child outgrew the behavior, becoming secure enough in his relationships that he no longer needed such tangible evidence of caring. So it was with Sheila.

One good thing came out of the incident with Mrs. Holmes' room. I tracked down Sheila's father. After school one evening in early February Anton and I piled into the car and drove out to the migrant camp. Sheila and her father lived in a small, tarpaper shack beside the railroad tracks.

He was a big man, over six feet tall, heavy-set with a huge belly that slopped over his belt, only one tooth on the bottom and very evil-smelling breath. When we arrived he was carrying a can of beer and was already quite drunk.

Anton forged ahead into the tiny house. It was only one room really, divided by a curtain. A lumpy brown couch was at one end and a bed was at the other. Otherwise there was no furniture. The place reeked of stale urine.

Sheila's father came into the house behind us and motioned us to sit on the couch. Sheila was crouched in a far corner by the bed, her eyes round and wild. She had failed to acknowledge either Anton or me, but sat folded in upon herself as she had in the first days of school. I mentioned that perhaps it would be best if Sheila were not present, as I needed to discuss some things with her father that might be painful for her to listen to.

He shook his head and flapped a hand in Sheila's direction. "She's gotta stay in that corner. You can't trust that kid out of your sight for five minutes. She tried to set fire to a place down the road the other night. If I don't keep her in, the police will be here again." He went on to give us the details.

"She ain't really my child," he explained, offering Anton a beer. "That bitch of a woman who's her mother, that's her bastard. She ain't my child and you can tell it. Just look at her. And the kid don't have a decent bone in her body. I haven't in all my born days seen a child like that one for causing trouble."

Anton and I listened speechlessly. I was mortified for her sake that Sheila was in the room. If he told her these things every day, no wonder she had such a low opinion of herself. At least, though, it was private. To tell it to us in front of her—I was horrified even to be there. It was like some scene out of a poorly written novel. Anton made an effort to refute the man's view but that only made him angry with us. So we let him talk, fearful of bringing repercussions on Sheila if we upset him.

"Now Jimmie, he was my boy. Better little boy you

96

never seen than my Jimmie. And that bitch, she took him. Just upped and took him right out from under my nose, she did. And what did she do? She leaves this little bastard." He sighed. "I told her if one more school person came out here about her, I wouldn't forget it."

"I didn't come to say anything bad," I said quickly. "She's doing a nice job in our room."

He snorted. "She should. With a class full of crazies, she should know how to act. Jesus Christ, woman, I'm at my wit's end with that child."

The conversation never improved. My blood was icy with horror and I wished I could shrink up and fall through a crack in the floor to save Sheila from the humiliation of having people she cared about hear his words. But I couldn't, nor could I stop him. Her father went on and on. I tried to tell him that Sheila was a gifted child with marvelous intelligence. That was not in his world. What did she need with that, he asked, it'd only give her more of a chance to think up trouble. Finally the conversation turned back to his beloved, lost Jimmie. He began to cry, big tears rolling over his fat cheeks. Where, oh where, had Jimmie been taken, and why had he been left with this little bogie that he did not even believe was his child?

In a detached way I felt sorry for the man. I think he did love the boy and the loss must have been difficult. In his tangled, immature way he seemed to see Sheila as somehow to blame for losing Jimmie. If she hadn't been so impossible perhaps his woman would have stayed. He did not know what to do with Sheila or himself. So he lost himself in a couple six-packs of beer and wept to two complete strangers about a life thirty years out of control.

As wretched as Sheila's life looked, I knew we would have a difficult time getting her removed from her father's care. This was a community with a huge population of losers. The migrants, the penitentiary, the state hospital, all combined to make a town within a town, one that was so large that the parent community could not meet its needs. There were not enough social workers and foster homes and welfare checks to sort out the disasters and repair the damage. Only the most severely abused children were removed from their homes because there was no place to put the others. Yet I felt compelled to ask her father if he had considered voluntary foster placement since he was having such a hard time.

My question was a mistake. From tears, he exploded into a rage, leaping up and waving his hands at me. Who was I to suggest he give his child up? What kind of person was I? He had never accepted help from anyone before; he was man enough to solve his own problems without any help from me, thank you. With that he demanded that Anton and I leave his house immediately. Filled with frustration and angry sorrow, we left hoping we had not endangered Sheila. It was a grim visit and I wished I had never gone.

Afterwards, I rode across the migrant camp to Anton's. He too lived in little more than a hut. There were three rooms which he shared with his wife and two young sons. It seemed pitifully inadequate to someone with my middle-class upbringing, but it was clean and well-kept. The Spartan furniture was offset by handmade rugs and needlepoint pillows. A large crucifix adorned a wall in the main room. Anton's wife was cheerful and welcoming, even though she spoke no English and I spoke no Spanish. His boys were eager, chattery little fellows who climbed all over me asking about the classroom their daddy had told them of. They were so verbal and spirited despite their youth that they seemed to be geniuses in my eyes. I had grown so used to viewing my kids as normal. The five of us shared three Cokes and a bowl of corn chips while Anton diffidently asked about the possibilities of his going back to school and earning a teaching degree. He did not even have a high school diploma yet, although he eagerly told me that he was studying for his General Equivalency Diploma. I had not previously heard about these secret dreams he had been nursing. He had grown to love the children in our class, in spite of his initial reluctance, and someday he hoped he might teach in a class of his own. I was touched by his dreams, because that indeed was what I feared they were. I doubted he was aware of all the time and money involved in attaining that level of education. But watching his wife beam as her husband talked of such great plans and seeing the little boys dance at the thought that their daddy was going to be a real teacher and someday they might live in a real house and have bicycles, I did not mention the drawbacks. Besides, my emotions had not fully recovered and my mind still wandered across to the other side of the camp, wondering what was happening in the shack by the railroad tracks.

CHAPTER 10

DURING THE TWO HOURS THAT SHEILA AND I had alone together, after school, I had begun reading aloud to her. Although she was perfectly capable of reading most of the books herself, I wanted to provide her with some extra closeness as well as share some of my favorite books with her. We also needed to talk about some of the things in the books, I found out, because Sheila had had such a deprived childhood that she did not understand many things. This was not because she did not know what the words meant, but because she had no idea how they applied to real life.

For instance, in *Charlotte's Web* Sheila puzzled the longest time over why the little girl wanted to keep the runt pig, Wilbur, in the first place. He was a runt after all, the poorest of the litter. In Sheila's mind it was perfectly understandable that the father did not want to keep him. I explained that Fern loved him because he was tiny and could not help being a runt. But Sheila could not conceptualize that. She lived strictly by the law of survival of the fittest.

So I read to her, holding her on my lap as we sat in the reading corner surrounded by pillows. When she did not understand a word or a passage, we talked about it, often wandering off into long discussions about the way things were. I was fascinated by this girl who possessed a child's innocence in reasoning and a child's directness, but an adult's comprehension. Her clear-eyed perception of things was in many ways frightening because it was so often nakedly right. But the child's way she put some things together made me laugh.

One night I brought in a copy of *The Little Prince*. "Hey Sheil," I called to her. "I've got a book to share with you."

She came running across the room, leaping squarely onto my stomach and snatching the book from my hands. Carefully she inspected all the pictures before we settled down to read. Once started, she sat motionless, her fingers gripping the cloth of my jeans.

The Little Prince is a short book and within half an hour I was almost halfway through it. When we came to the part about the fox she became even more intent. I could feel her bony little hips in my lap as she wiggled to become more comfortable.

"Come and play with me," proposed the little prince. "I am so unhappy."

"I cannot play with you," the fox said. "I am not tamed."

"Ah! Please excuse me," said the little prince. But, after some thought, he added:

"What does that mean—'tame'?"

* * *

"It is an act too often neglected," said the fox. "It means to establish ties."

" 'To establish ties'?"

"Just that," said the fox. "To me, you are still nothing more than a little boy who is just like a hundred thousand other little boys. And I have no need of you. And you, on your part, have no need of me. To you, I am nothing more than a fox like a hundred thousand other foxes. But if you tame me, then we shall need each other. To me, you will be unique in all the world. To you, I shall be unique in all the world . . ."

* * *

"My life is very monotonous," he said. "I hunt chickens; men hunt me. All the chickens are just alike, and all the men are just alike. And, in consequence, I am a little bored. But if you tame me, it will be as if the sun came to shine on my life. I shall know the sound of a step that will be different from all the others. Other steps send me hurrying back underneath the ground. Yours will call me, like music, out of my burrow. And then look: You see the grain-fields down yonder? I do not eat bread. Wheat is of no use to me. The wheat fields have nothing to say to me. And that is sad. But you have hair that is the color of gold. Think how wonderful that will be when you have tamed me! The grain, which is also golden, will bring me back the thought of you. And I shall love to listen to the wind in the wheat . . ."

The fox gazed at the little prince, for a long time.

"Please—tame me!" he said.

"I want to, very much," the little prince replied. "But I have not much time. I have friends to discover, and a great many things to understand."

"One only understands the things that one tames," said the fox. "Men have no more time to understand anything. They buy things all ready made at the shops. But there is no shop anywhere where one can buy friendship, and so men have no friends any more. If you want a friend, tame me . . ."

"What must I do, to tame you?" asked the little prince.

"You must be very patient," replied the fox. "First you will sit down at a little distance from me—like that—in the grass. I shall look at you out of the corner of my eye, and you will say nothing. Words are the source of misunderstandings. But you will sit a little closer to me every day . . ."

Sheila put her hand on the page. "Read that again, okay?"

I reread the section. She twisted around in my lap to look at me and for a long time locked me in her gaze. "That be what you do, huh?"

"What do you mean?"

"That's what you done with me, huh? Tamed me."

I smiled.

"It be just like this book says, remember? I do be so

scared and I run in the gym and then you come in and you sit on the floor. Remember that? And I peed my pants, remember? I be so scared. I think you gonna whip me fierce bad 'cause I done so much wrong that day. But you sit on the floor. And you come a little closer and a little closer. You was taming me, huh?"

I smiled in disbelief. "Yeah, I guess maybe I was."

"You tame me. Just like the little prince tames the fox. Just like you tamed me. And now I be special to you, huh? Just like the fox."

"Yeah, you're special all right, Sheil."

She turned back around, settling into my lap again. "Read the rest of it."

So the little prince tamed the fox. And when the hour of his departure drew near—

"Ah," said the fox, "I shall cry."

"It is your own fault," said the little prince. "I never wished you any sort of harm; but you wanted me to tame you . . ."

"Yes, that is so," said the fox.

"But now you are going to cry!" said the little prince.

"Yes, that is so," said the fox.

"Then it has done you no good at all!"

"It has done me good," said the fox, "because of the color of the wheat fields." And then he added:

"Go and look again at the roses. You will understand now that yours is unique in all the world. Then come back to say goodbye to me, and I will make you a present of a secret."

The little prince went away, to look again at the roses.

"You are not at all like my rose," he said. "As yet you are nothing. No one has tamed you, and you have tamed no one. You are like my fox when first I knew him. He was only a fox like a hundred thousand other foxes. But I have made him my friend, and now he is unique in all the world."

And the roses were very much embarrassed.

"You are beautiful, but you are empty," he went on. "One could not die for you. To be sure, an ordinary passerby would think that my rose looked just like you—the rose that belongs to me. But in herself alone she is more important than all the hundreds of you other roses: because it is she that I have sheltered behind the screen; because it is for her that I have killed the caterpillars (except the two or three that we saved to become butterflies); because it is she that I have listened to, when she grumbled, or boasted, or even sometimes when she said nothing. Because she is *my* rose."

And he went back to meet the fox.

"Goodbye," he said.

"Goodbye," said the fox. "And now here is my secret, a very simple secret: It is only with the heart that one can see rightly; what is essential is invisible to the eye."

"What is essential is invisible to the eye," the little prince repeated, so that he would be sure to remember.

"It is the time you have wasted for your rose that makes your rose so important."

"It is the time I have wasted for my rose—" said the little prince, so that he would be sure to remember.

"Men have forgotten this truth," said the fox. "But you must not forget it. You become responsible, forever, for what you have tamed. You are responsible for your rose . . ."

Sheila slid off my lap and turned around, getting on her knees so that she could look directly into my eyes. "You be 'sponsible for me. You tame me, so now you be 'sponsible for me?"

For several moments I looked into her fathomless eyes. I was not certain what she was asking me. She reached up and put her arms around my neck, not releasing me from her gaze.

"I tame you a little bit too, huh? You tame me and I tame you. And now I do be 'sponsible for you too, huh?"

I nodded. She let go of me and sat down. For a moment she lost herself, tracing a design on the rug with her finger.

"Why you do this?" she asked.

"Do what, Sheil?"

"Tame me."

I did not know what to say.

Her water blue eyes rose to me. "Why you care? I can't never figure that out. Why you *want* to tame me?"

My mind raced. They had never told me in my education classes or my child-psych classes that there would be children like this one. I was unprepared. This seemed like one of those moments when if I could only say the right thing . . .

"Well, kiddo, I don't have a good reason, I guess. It just seemed like the thing to do."

"Do it be like the fox? Do I be special now 'cause you tame me? Do I be a special girl?"

I smiled. "Yeah, you're my special girl. It's like the fox says, now that I made you my friend, you're unique in all the world. I guess I always wanted you for my special girl. I guess that's why I tamed you to begin with."

"Do you love me?"

I nodded.

"I love you too. You be my special best person in the whole world."

Sheila scrunched herself down and around, lying on the carpet with her head resting on my thigh. She fiddled with a piece of lint she had found on the floor. I prepared to read again.

"Torey?"

"Yes?"

"You ain't never gonna leave me?"

I touched her bangs brushing them back. "Well, someday, I reckon. When the school year is over and you go on to another class and another teacher. But not before then and that's a long time away."

She shot up. "You be my teacher. I ain't never gonna have another teacher."

"I'm your teacher now. But someday we'll be finished."

She shook her head; her eyes had clouded. "This here be my room. And I do be gonna be in here forever."

"It won't be for a long time yet. When the time comes, you'll be ready."

"No sir. You tame me; you be 'sponsible for me. You can't never leave me cause you be 'sponsible for me forever. It says so right there, and that's what you done to me, so it's your fault that I got tame."

"Hey honey," I pulled her into my lap. "Don't worry about it."

"But you gonna leave me," she said accusingly, pulling out of my hold. "Just like my Mama done. And Jimmie. And everybody. My Pa, he would if they wouldn't put him in jail for it. He told me that. You do be just like everybody else. You leave me too. Even after you tame me and I not ask you to."

"It won't be that way, Sheila. I'm not leaving you. I'm staying right here. When the year is over things will change, but I won't leave you. Just like it says in the story, the little prince tamed the fox and now he's gone, but really he's always going to be with the fox because every time the fox sees the wheat fields he thinks of the little prince. He remembers how much the little prince loved him. That's how it'll be with us. We'll always love each other. Going away is easier then, because every time you remember someone who loves you, you feel a little bit of their love."

"No you don't. You just miss them."

I reached an arm out to her, bringing her close once again. She wasn't going to be convinced. "Well, it's a little too hard to think about right now. You're not ready to leave and I won't leave you. Someday you will be ready and it'll be easier."

"No, I won't. I won't never be ready."

I was rocking her in my arms, holding her very tightly. This was too scary a thing for her right now. I did not know how to treat the issue because the time would come when she would have to leave, either when the state hospital had an opening or at the end of the school year in June. I already suspected my class would not exist the next year for a number of reasons. There was no use hoping that I would have her beyond the end of the year. So the time was coming and I did not know if in four short months she would feel much differently than she did right now.

Sheila let me rock her. She was studying my face. "Will you cry?"

"When?"

"When you leave?"

"Remember what the fox said? 'One runs the risk of weeping, if one lets himself be tamed.' He's right. One cries a little. Every time someone goes away, you cry a little. Love hurts sometimes. Sometimes it makes you cry."

"I cry about Jimmie and my Mama. But my Mama, she don't love me none."

"I don't know about that. That happened before I knew you and I never met your Mama. But I can't imagine that she didn't love you some. It's very hard not to love your kids."

"But she left me on the highway. You don't do that to your kids if you love them. Pa, he tell me that."

"Like I said, Sheila, I don't know. I don't know who's right. But it isn't always that way. I'm never going to leave you in that way. When school is over and you go somewhere else, we'll still be together, even if we don't see each other. Because like the fox said, every time he saw a wheat field he thought of the little prince. So in a special way the little prince was with him. That's the way it'll be with us."

"I don't want no wheat fields. I want you."

"But that's special too, Sheil. At first we'll be a little sad, but it'll get better and then it'll be good. Every time we think of the other, we will feel nice inside. You see, there won't ever be enough miles to make us forget how happy we've been. Nothing can take away your memories."

She pushed her face into me. "I don't want to think about it."

"No, you're right. This isn't the time to worry about it. It's a long ways away. In the meantime, we'll think of other things."

CHAPTER 11

ALTHOUGH I HAD CEASED TO BE OBSESSED
with our paperwork war, it was never completely out of
my mind. First, I had a hard time keeping Sheila busy
without needing one of the adults with her constantly. I
also worried that she would not be acceptable to a regular
class teacher if she would never do any worksheets or
workbooks. While in my class we could get away with it, a
regular teacher with twenty-five other children and an
academic schedule to keep would never be able to afford
such frivolity. Finally, I worried that she was finding out
that her current method kept a lot of adult attention fo-
cused on her. She was perfectly capable of answering almost any question we thought up for her, but she thrived
on capturing Anton, Whitney or me and reciting her answers. This was not particularly acceptable behavior even
in my room.

I still had no firm idea why she was so negative about
paperwork. I suspect that it had something to do with failure. If she never committed anything to paper, it was impossible to prove that she ever made a mistake. And
Sheila fell apart when she did make an error and was cor-
rected, regardless of how gentle the correction was. I

had an awful suspicion from random comments she made that once she had taken a paper home and had had a bad encounter with her father regarding it. But she had a large number of bad encounters with him, so I doubted that that alone accounted for her phobia. Perhaps she simply was bright enough to figure out that this method saved her a lot of work and got her the attention she craved. I did not usually think that, because there were a lot of easier ways for a bright child to achieve the same end. After a particularly hectic day, though, Anton expressed those sentiments.

However, there was one thing Sheila seemed to be finding more and more irresistible. I encouraged a great amount of creative writing in class. The children kept journals in which they recorded what they felt, things that happened to them and other important events in their lives. Often when I tangled with a child and one or both of us got angry, the child had learned that one place for expression was in the journal. Thus, kids were scribbling in their journals on and off all day. Each night I went through and left notes or comments to the children about what they had written. It was a personal communication and we each valued the opportunity to find out how the other felt. In a similar manner I had formal writing assignments almost daily in which the children wrote on an assigned topic. I had found that after the children learned to write easily and to associate words with the feelings they could evoke, all of them, even Susannah, could express themselves in some instances better on paper than face-to-face. So in our room a great amount of written correspondence took place.

Needless to say, Sheila, with her distaste for paper, did not write. This seemed to bother her a bit. She would crane her neck to see what the other kids were writing, or wander close to them during creative writing time, instead of going over to the reading corner or somewhere to play as she was supposed to. Finally, a day came in mid-February when her curiosity got the better of her.

She came over to me after I had handed out the sheets for writing. "I might write something, if you give me a piece of paper."

I looked down at her. It occurred to me that I might be able to swing the whole paperwork issue around to my side with a little reverse psychology. So I shook my head. "No, this is paperwork. You don't do paperwork, remember?"

"I might do this."

"No, I don't think so. I can't risk wasting any more paper on you. You wouldn't like it anyway. You go play. That's more fun."

She wandered away for a few moments. Then she came back. I was leaning over William helping him spell a word. Sheila tugged on my belt. "I wanna do it, Torey."

I shook my head. "No, you don't. Not really."

"Yes, I do."

Ignoring her, I went back to William.

"I won't waste no paper."

"Sheila, writing is for kids who do paperwork. Now you don't do it, so writing isn't for you."

"I could do some paperwork. A little bit, maybe, if I could have a piece of paper to write on."

I shook my head. "No, you don't like it. You've told me that yourself. You don't have to do it. Go play now, so I can help William."

She remained standing beside me. After a few moments of not getting results, she went and asked Anton. "Torey's got the paper," he said, pointing in my direction. "You'll have to ask her."

"She won't give me none."

He shrugged and rolled his big brown eyes. "Well, then I'm sorry for you. I don't have any paper you can use."

Sheila came back to me. She was getting angry with me and trying not to show it. "I want you to give me a piece of paper, Torey. Now, gimme it."

I raised an eyebrow in warning.

She gave a frustrated stomp with one foot and shoved out her lower lip. I bent back over William.

She changed tactics. "Please? Please? I won't wreck it. I won't tear it up. Cross my heart and hope to die. Please?"

I regarded her. "I can't believe you. Maybe if you do some papers for me tomorrow and I see you don't tear them up, then I'll give you writing paper during creative writing tomorrow afternoon."

"I want it now, Torey."

"I know you do. But you show me I can trust you and

you can have some tomorrow. We're almost out of time today anyhow."

She eyed me carefully, trying to determine a way to make me give in. "If you give me paper I'll write something you don't know about me. I'll write you something secret."

"You write me something secret tomorrow."

At that she gave a grunt of anger and stalked off across the room to the other table. She pulled out a chair very loudly and sat down with great emphasis. Little snorts punctuated the air. I smiled inwardly. She was cute when she was mad, now that she was learning to handle it more appropriately. Giving me absolutely black stares, she remained at the other table.

After a few moments I wandered over in her direction. "I suppose, if you write fast, I could give you a piece of paper today."

She looked up expectantly.

"Except you can't tear it up."

"I won't."

"What will we do if you do tear it up?"

"I won't. I said I won't. I promise."

"Are you going to do other papers for me, if I give you this one?"

She nodded emphatically.

"You'll do your math paper?"

She frowned in exasperation. "I ain't gonna have no time left if you keep talking to me all day."

I grinned and handed her a piece of paper. "This better be a good secret."

Clutching the paper in both hands she scurried over to the other table to grab a felt-tipped pen. She had been eyeing the pens for some time and now with both the pen and the hard-earned paper she darted off to the far side of the room. Scrambling under the rabbit's cage, she began to write.

She *was* fast. Somehow I had expected her to have difficulty since she had not written in so long. But as in so many other ways, Sheila surprised me. Within minutes she was back, the piece of paper folded into a tiny square. She sidled up next to me when I wasn't looking and pressed it into my hand.

"This here be a secret now. You don't go showing it to nobody. It do be just for you."

"Okay." I began unfolding it.

"No, don't read it now. Save it."

Nodding, I slipped the little square of paper into my pocket.

I forgot about it until that night when I was changing for bed. Then the folded square fell out onto the floor. Carefully I picked it up and straightened it out. Inside, written in blue felt-tip, I found what must have been for Sheila, with all her dignity, a very personal note.

A special thing I want you to know but not tell Nobody

You know sometimes the kids make Fun of me and call me names and befor I used not to put on clene Close. But sometimes I dont cos you know what I do but please dont tell I wet the bed. I dont mean to Pa he wips me for it if he knows but He dont mostly. I just don't know why Torey I try real hard to Stop. You wouldnt be mad at me would you. My pa he is but I dont mean to Honest. it bothers me alot but it Make me ashamed of myself. Pa he says Im a baby but I be 7 soon when I do then there aint no clene underpanz and the kids make fun of me. Please dont tell no kids about this ok. Or dont tell Mr Colinz. or Anton or Whiteney or anybody ok. I just want you to know.

I read the note through, touched by her openness and amazed by her writing ability. By and large the note was well-written, punctuated and spelled correctly. It puzzled me that she used "I'm," since I did not ever remember hearing her say it. I smiled to myself and sat down and wrote her a note back.

So the first break in the paperwork war had been made. The next day with help she managed to do a math paper. It was carefully done and I suggested it go up on the bulletin board where I displayed all the children's good work. This was too much for Sheila and I later found the math paper shredded in the trash can. I was more careful after that. She became able to do two or three written assignments without supervision. Occasionally she would slip

112

back and destroy the paper partway through the assignment or after completing it, especially those that were difficult for her. But if I gave her a second sheet, she would try again. I never marked anything wrong because Sheila had such a tenuous hold on herself in committing her work to paper. It was far too fragile at that point to take any criticism, however well-meaning the critic's intentions. Instead, Anton or I always checked on her while she did the papers and discussed some alternatives to questions she was answering incorrectly. Otherwise I kept a low profile on her increasing ability to do this task. It was not that important a matter, despite what my teacher's instinct told me, and I never wanted her to feel that I measured her worth by how many papers she did. Obviously someone had already communicated that to her and I wanted it clear that that was not true in our classroom. Regardless of how inconvenient her distrust of paperwork had been, she needed to know that nobody would be valued less than a stack of school papers.

Interestingly enough, Sheila found great outlet in creative writing. In this area the old fears seemed to drop away, and she wrote spontaneously and copiously. Line after line of her loose, rather sloppy writing would hurry across the page telling about things that often seemed too personal to say face-to-face. I could usually count on five or six extra pages in the correction basket each night.

I never learned whatever it was that motivated Sheila toward her paper phobia. Later interactions with her over it and later comments that she made reaffirmed my belief that it was related to a fear of failure. But I never really knew. Nor did I feel a pressing need to know, only because so few human behaviors can be reduced to such simple cause-effect terms. There were more important things to worry about, things more important than ferreting out a mysterious and ultimately academic "why."

Allan, the school psychologist, returned shortly after Valentine's Day with a whole battery of tests for Sheila, including a Stanford-Binet IQ test. I balked a bit when I met him and his armload in the office that morning. I knew to my satisfaction that Sheila was a gifted child; she proved it daily. What difference did it make if her IQ were 170 or 175 or 180? It was all so far beyond normal that the numbers were meaningless. Even a variation of thirty points did not matter much. I would not know how to handle her any differently if she had an IQ of 150 or 180; she was too discrepant. But I suspect Allan was excited over finding such an interesting specimen and wanted to test her more for his own education than for any added benefit to Sheila. I relented because I knew the time was coming when we would have to face the authorities who had committed her to the state hospital. She certainly did not belong there; I could see that beyond a doubt now. I was hoping all the illustrious IQ scores would serve us in the end.

She topped out the Stanford-Binet as she had done on the other tests. An extrapolated score gave her an IQ of 182. As I looked at it, I was affected in a mystical way; 182 is beyond anyone's comprehension. That is as far in the direction of genius as an IQ of 18 is in the direction of retardation. And everyone knows how very different from the normal population a child with an 18 IQ is. What people generally fail to realize is that a child with a 182 is just as different.

What moved me most was considering how she ever came to possess that kind of knowledge. It almost seemed to me as if it were some sort of anomaly like brain damage in reverse. Her father—if he was, indeed, her father —was of normal intelligence and from what I could make out, so was her mother. Where in Sheila's abused, deprived six years had she learned what words like "chattel" meant? How had that happened? It seemed as nearly impossible to me as anything I had ever encountered. I was flooded with thoughts that she must be proof of reincarnation. I could see no other explanation for this extraordinary child.

Almost before I realized what I was thinking, a second emotion entered into the mystery. In the back of my head I heard the chant of a TV commerical I had seen once: "A mind is a terrible thing to waste." My gut tightened. There was so much to do with this child, and so little time. I did not know if it would be nearly enough.

CHAPTER 12

THE LAST WEEK IN FEBRUARY I WAS SPEAK-
ing at a conference out of state. I had known about the
engagement since before school had started in the fall and
had reminded Ed Somers periodically that I was still planning to attend. Now as the time grew near, I once again
called Ed to make arrangements for my replacement.

The children had been with a substitute earlier in the
year in November when I had gone to a workshop. It was
only one day and I had prepared the kids, so things had
gone well. I felt it was very important that they have these
little tests of independence. Regardless of how much progress they had made during their year with me, it would be
futile if they only performed reliably in my presence. I
had seen more good teachers fail because of this problem
than any other and was haunted by the thought that I
might fall prey to that difficulty. I suppose what worried
me was that I tended to form a closer, more intense relationship with my kids than did a number of teachers in
the same general area as I. When I saw them breeding
dependency in their more detached manners, I feared I
was in trouble. Thus far, I hadn't been, but I took every
opportunity to let my children cope without me.

115

Sheila worried me though. She had not been with us very long yet and was still quite dependent. I saw this as a natural stage for her at the time, but I worried that my leaving, even for a short period of time, might frighten her.

On the Monday before my absence, which would be Thursday and Friday of that week, I mentioned casually to the children that I would be gone. Again on Tuesday, I mentioned it. On neither occasion did Sheila appear to attend to the comment. But on Wednesday after lunch I sat the kids down for a discussion. I explained I would be gone the next two days and not in the room. Anton would be there and so would Whitney and there would be a substitute teacher. Things would go just as always and there was no need to worry. I would be back on the next Monday when we were all going on a field trip to the fire station. We discussed ways of behaving properly around a substitute teacher; things that would make the job easier for her and things that should not be done. We role-played how to talk to her and how to deal with the minor crises that always seemed to crop up with subs. Everyone participated actively in the discussion. Everyone but Sheila. As the reality of what I was saying dawned on her, she regarded me anxiously. Her hand went up.

"Yes, Sheila?"

"You gonna be gone?"

"Yes, I am. That's what this is all about. I won't be here tomorrow or Friday, but I'll be back on Monday. That's what we're talking about."

"You gonna be gone?"

"Jeepers, Sheila," Peter said, "you deaf or something? What you think we been doing all this time?"

"You gonna be gone?"

I nodded. The other kids were looking at her strangely.

"You ain't gonna be here?"

"I'll be back on Monday. Just two days and then I'll be back."

Her face clouded over, her eyes filling with wary concern. She rose to her feet and retreated backwards toward the housekeeping corner, watching me the entire time.

I went on to answer other questions and finally broke up the group when it seemed everyone was satisfied. It was almost time for recess and then cooking.

Sheila remained in the housekeeping corner fiddling aimlessly with toy pots and pans. Anton called her to get her coat on for recess but she refused to come, popping her thumb into her mouth and looking defiantly at him. I motioned to Anton to go out with the others and went over to her. Turning a chair around backwards, I straddled it, resting my chin on the back.

"You're upset with me, aren't you?"

"You never tell me you go away."

"Yes, I did, Sheil. Both Monday and yesterday in morning discussion."

"But you didn't tell me."

"I told everybody."

She threw a tin pan down so that it clattered. "It ain't fair you go leave me. I don't want you to."

"I know you don't and I'm sorry for your sake that I have to. But I am coming back, Sheila. I'll only be gone for two days."

"I ain't never, never gonna like you again. I ain't never gonna do anything you ask. You do be so mean to me. You tame me so's I like you and then you leave. You ain't supposed to do that, don't you know? That be what my Mama done and that ain't a good thing to do to little kids. They put you in jail for leaving little kids. My Pa, he says so."

"Sheila, it's different from that."

"I ain't gonna listen to you. I ain't never gonna listen to you again. I liked you and you be mean to me. You are gonna go away and leave me and you said you wouldn't. That be a fierce awful thing to do to a kid you tame. Don't you know that?"

"Sheila, listen to me . . ."

"I ain't never gonna listen to you. Don't you hear me say that?" Her voice was almost inaudible, but pregnant with feeling. "I hate you."

I looked at her. She kept her face averted. For the first time since she had come I saw her bring a finger up to one eye to stop an unfallen tear. In panic she pressed her fingers tight against her temples, willing the tears back. "Look what you make me do," she muttered accusingly. "You make me cry and I don't want to. You know I don't like to cry. I hate you more than anybody and I ain't never gonna be nice in here again. No matter what."

117

For a single moment the tears glistened in her eyes. They never fell. She darted past me, grabbed her jacket and ran out the door to the playground.

I got my own jacket and joined the children. Sheila sat by herself in the very farthest corner. Hunched up against the chilly February wind, she sat with her face hidden in her arms.

"Not taking it so well, eh?" Anton said.

"Nope, she's not taking it so well."

After recess when the other children readied for cooking, Sheila remained in the housekeeping corner idly clattering toys around. I let her be. She was upset and had reason to be. Despite her isolation from us, she was handling her distress quite well. No tantrums, no destruction, no bolting. I was surprised and pleased with the manner in which she was coping. Sheila had come a long way in two months.

The other kids tried to coax Sheila into joining them. Tyler, ever the class mother, fussed over Sheila until Whitney told her to get back to the cookies. Peter kept asking why she was standing there and not joining us. I explained that Sheila was feeling a little angry just then and was keeping herself in control by not being with us.

After the cookies were done and everyone sat around eating, I joined William and Guillermo. Tyler had taken some cookies over to Sheila, who was still in retreat midst the dolls and dishes of the housekeeping corner. Guillermo was showing me a new Braille watch his grandfather had given him and he and William were testing me to see if I could read it with my eyes closed.

"Torey," Sarah shouted from the other side of the room, "come here, Sheila's throwing up."

Peter bounced over in delighted glee. "Sheila just puked all over everything." Peter loved gruesome catastrophes.

Anton went for the janitor and I went back to see what had happened. The other kids gathered around like we had a three-ring circus.

I lifted Sheila out of the area and set her down beside me. Pushing back her bangs, I felt her forehead. She wasn't hot.

"Maybe she's got a virus," Peter said. "Last year I

puked about a million times one night and all over my bed and stuff, and my mom said I had a virus."

"No," I replied. "I don't think Sheila's sick. I think she's just a little nervous about things today and it got to her tummy."

"That happened to me once. My uncle was coming and I got really excited," William said. "And I got sick because of it. He was going to take me fishing."

Peter snorted. "I bet it was Tyler's cookies."

"I think it would help if everybody would clear out of here and go sit down someplace," I said.

When Anton returned, I took Sheila into the bathroom to clean her up. She was compliant but refused to look at me or to speak. So in silence I washed off her face and clothes.

"Do you think you might throw up again?" I asked.

No response.

"Sheil, cut that out. Now answer me. I asked how you were feeling. Are you going to be sick again?"

"I didn't mean to."

"I know you didn't. But I wanted to know if you thought you were still feeling sick, so we could be prepared if we needed to be. It's almost time to go home."

"My bus don't come 'til five."

"I think it would be better if you went home when school's out. They sort of have a rule about throwing up at school. They wouldn't want you on the bus. And I just think it'd be better for you to go home. Anton can take you after school."

"But I didn't mean to. I won't do it again."

"Honey, that's not the point."

"You hate me. You hate me and won't even be nice to me when I be sick. You do be such a mean person."

I rolled my eyes in exasperation. "Sheila, I do not hate you. Honestly, what can I do to get through to you that I am coming back? I will only be gone tomorrow and Friday. Just two short days. Then I'll be back. Don't you understand that?"

I was frustrated. She was a bright child, she knew how long two days were. Yet she stood there uncomprehending. I doubted her vomiting was any more than a physical reaction to emotional distress, but I did not know what to do with her. She would not hear what I was saying.

Rising from where I had been washing her off, I shook my head. Then I shrugged. "Do you want me to rock you a little while until school gets out? Maybe that will help settle your tummy some."

She shook her head.

The janitor was just leaving and the children were starting to get ready to go home. Anton looked questioningly in my direction. I spread my hands in a gesture of bewilderment.

The other kids were getting their coats on, and Sheila stood in the bathroom doorway and watched. When I looked at her, she seemed a little pale. Perhaps I had been too hasty in judging, perhaps it was a virus. But I didn't think so. There had been too many nervous stomachs in my experience. She was, after all, struggling with a hard thing.

I sat down in the rocking chair and turned in her direction. She remained in the doorway. The distance seemed so far between us. How fragile the bond was that held us. Uppermost in my mind was the frustration of being unable to convince her that I, unlike all the others, was not abandoning her. However, underneath the frustration blossomed such admiration for this child. She was so strong and courageous. There was no reason why she should suspect I was being honest with her. Nothing in her past gave her grounds to think that I would return, and she was doing the only sensible thing. Yet as she stood in the doorway watching me, a pantomime of self-doubt and fear and sorrow played across her face. She was trying so hard to believe me, the war between her experience and her dreams vivid in her eyes. I was filled with respect for her, such heart-grinding, unspeakable respect, because she was trying so hard. This was one of those moments that made all the others worthwhile. We were touching each other's souls.

I reached a hand out. "Come here, kitten. Let me rock you."

She hesitated, then slowly approached. Without a word she climbed into my lap.

"This has been a hard day, hasn't it?"

She pressed her fingers to her temples.

"I know you don't understand what's happening, Sheila. You don't understand how I can do this to you and still

120

like you." I rocked her, pushing back her bangs and feeling the silky softness of her hair. "You're just going to have to trust me."

Her body was rigid against mine, like it had been in the beginning. She did not relax. "You tamed me. I didn't ask you to, but you did. Now you leave. It ain't fair. You be 'sponsible for me. You said so yourself."

I puzzled over her sudden change to the past tense. I had never heard it except in rare, random instances. "Kitten, please trust me. I'll be back. It won't be so bad as you think. Anton will still be here, and Whitney. And the substitute will be real nice, I just know it. You'll have fun if you just give yourself the chance."

She did not answer, but simply sat, her fingers white against her temples. There wasn't any more to say. She did not believe me or else she could not bring herself to admit she did. I was too used to her verbal ability. I sometimes forgot she was a six-year-old child. I forgot how many problems she had and how short a time she had been with us. I was expecting too much in wanting her to understand.

The conference was in a West Coast state which had a milder February climate. Chad went with me and we spent most of the time on the beach walking in the surf. It was a marvelous change. I seldom realized how tied up with the children I was until a moment like this occurred and I got away. My interactions were intense and all-consuming for me. When I was working, I could never perceive how tense the involvement left me. Now, on the sunny beach, I felt the weariness drain away.

It was a good conference and an even better vacation. I never thought of the children at all except in bed at night. Even then it was a hazy recollection. I knew they would take care of themselves in my absence. For Chad and me it was a spiritual rebirth. Since Sheila had come, proving such a challenge and forcing me to take my planning home at night, Chad had been slighted. He understood my fascination with the kids, but he still resented the fact that they absorbed every moment. Four days alone together left us happy and relaxed.

* * *

On Monday morning I returned, anxious to get back to work. We had the field trip to the fire station planned in the afternoon and I had to make last minute calls on arrangements and check with all the parents who had promised to help.

Anton met me in the hallway as I was returning from the phone. He bulged his eyes. "We had quite a time in your absence," he said.

I could tell from his tone of voice that the "time" had not been a good one and I feared to ask. "What happened?"

"Sheila went absolutely berserk. She refused to talk. She pulled all the stuff off the walls, all the books out of the bookcases. She gave Peter a bloody nose on Friday. She wouldn't do any work at all. I couldn't even get her to sit in her chair. On Thursday she broke the record player. And on Friday afternoon she tried to break the glass out of the door with her shoe."

"You're kidding!"

"Uh-uh. Jesus, Torey, I wish I was. She was a holy terror."

"Cripes," I muttered, "I thought she was getting over doing that kind of junk."

"She was worse than I've seen her in ages. She spent the whole time in the quiet corner, having to be held in the chair every moment of it. She was worse than she ever was when she came."

My heart sank. A vast cesspool of emotions gurgled unhappily within me. I had honestly believed I could trust her to behave while I was gone. It hurt to realize I had misguessed so badly. I felt like I had been personally insulted. I had trusted her; I had depended on her good behavior and she had let me down.

I planned to discuss the matter with her but her bus was late. The other kids began to arrive, all bearing tales. "You ought to have seen what Sheila done," Sarah said excitedly. "She wrecked the whole room."

"Yeah!" Guillermo chirped. "That substitute, Mrs. Markham, she spanked Sheila and made her sit in the quiet corner and Whitney had to hold her all afternoon, 'cause she wouldn't."

Peter bounced around me, his dark eyes blazing with delight. "And she was real mean to Whitney and Whitney

122

cried and then guess what? Even Mrs. Markham cried. And Sarah cried and Tyler cried. All the girls cried because Sheila was so naughty. But I didn't. I socked her. I hit her good for being so bad."

"Her bad," Max confirmed, twirling around me.

My dismal discouragement turned to anger. How could she have done this to me? She had apparently behaved worse than she ever had when I was there. I thought she should have had good enough control to make it for two days without my lurking about every minute. I was deeply disappointed; my confidence about handling her had reached an all-time low. She was getting back at me; she had behaved that way on purpose and all the time and effort I had given her had been to no avail.

Sheila arrived after we had started morning discussion. She regarded me suspiciously as she sat down. The familiar musty odor of stale urine wafted up. She hadn't even bothered to wash since I had left.

My own displeasure did not lessen when I saw her. I was feeling very defensive, believing that her behavior had been a direct assault on my credibility as a teacher. As with all the others with whom she had come into contact, she had figured out what was most important to me and had used it as revenge. The more I thought about it, the worse I felt. This was far harder for me to accept than the incident of the first day or even Mrs. Holmes' room, because it had been so directly aimed at me.

After discussion I called her over. We sat in chairs away from the others. "I hear you didn't handle yourself very well."

She stared at me, her feelings unreadable.

"I came back and all I heard was about the bad things you did. I want you to explain that to me."

She said nothing but met me with unwavering eyes.

"I'm mad at you, Sheila. I'm the maddest I've been in a long time. Now I want to hear why you did that."

Still no response.

Rage rose within me as I saw those cold, distant eyes. In sudden desperation I grabbed her shoulders and shook her roughly. "Speak to me, dammit! Speak to me!" But what emotion was there closed, and she gritted her teeth. Horrified at losing control of myself, I let go of her shoulders. God, this job was getting to be too much for me.

She remained in stony silence, glaring at me. My aggressiveness had brought up her own anger and she was an equal match for me, if not better. This was her world, this realm of physical force. She was more a master of it than I and I could tell I had made a mistake in touching her that way. I imagined that she could outlast any sort of physical devastation I was capable of and still not speak. But I was so full of disappointment. My shoulders sagged.

"I trusted you," I said, my voice soft, the discouragement undisguised. "I trusted you for two lousy days, Sheila. I trusted you, can't you see that? And you want to know how it makes me feel to come back and hear you behaved like that?"

Sheila exploded with a fury I had been unprepared for. "I never told you to trust me! I never said that; you did! I never said you could trust me. You can't! Nobody can trust me! I never said you could!" She tore off, careening frantically around the perimeter of the room before scuttling under the table the animal cages were on. Her distress was so great that she sat under the table emitting little strangled noises that were not exactly sobs or screams or words. But their emotion was clear enough.

Her response had surprised me and I sat in the chair without moving. The other children had paused to look at us, their concern mirrored in one another's eyes. I just sat and looked at her in her hiding place under the table. I did not know what to do.

"Well, then you're not going anywhere with us this afternoon, Sheila," I said at last. "I'm not taking anyone I can't trust. You can stay with Anton."

She crawled out from under the table. "I can too go."

"No, I'm afraid not. I can't trust you."

She looked horror stricken. I knew that the field trip meant a great deal to her. She loved going places with us. "I can too go."

I shook my head. "No, you can't."

Sheila screamed, letting loose high-pitched earsplitting shrieks. She still stood over by the animal cages and began leaping up and down, beating the air with her hands.

"Sheila, cut it out or over to the quiet corner. Right now."

She was clearly out of control. Flinging herself on the floor she banged her head violently on the ground. Anton made a flying leap toward her to intercept the self-destruction. Never before had she done such a thing; I had expected her to go off into one of her destructive rages and evidently so had the children who were covertly putting their valuables out of the way. But she had never attempted to hurt herself before. Some of the other kids, particularly Max and Susannah, would do that, but never Sheila.

Anton had her tight in his arms. She struggled savagely, all the while screaming. I couldn't hear myself think. Then as suddenly as it started, it stopped, the room falling into unearthly silence. I dashed over fearing that she had hurt herself to stop so abruptly. Anton released his grip on her and she melted through his arms like warm butter, slithering into a little lump on the carpet. Her arms were over her head, her face into the tweed of the rug.

"Are you all right, Sheila?" I asked.

She turned her head. "Please let me go," she whispered.

After that terrible show of emotion I was alarmed. "I don't think you'd better." If she were behaving like this I was fearful of controlling her outside the room.

"I do be sorry for what I done. Let me go. You can trust me. Please?" Her voice was very small. "Gimme a chance. I'll show you how good I can be. Please? I wanna go."

I looked down at her. My own feelings were returning and I was beginning to think all that violent behavior was a con because she had stopped it so fast. That renewed some of my anger. "I don't think so, Sheila. Maybe next time."

She began screaming again, covering her face with her hands but remaining on the floor. She looked like a rag doll in the contorted position she lay in. I turned and walked away to work with the other children.

All morning she lay in a lump on the floor. She screamed for a while longer and then fell into silence, not moving, not looking up from her huddle. At first I was tempted to move her to the quiet corner, but I changed my mind. I was feeling defeated; I did not want to tangle with her.

By lunch my spirits had flagged completely. I was beginning to realize that I had been angry with her for exposing what I perceived as a teaching deficit in myself. I was mad because I was not able to leave her successfully. I was angry because she had done to me what I had watched her do to so many others. Somehow, I had honestly believed she would never take revenge against me. She had not until then and I had enough of an inflated ego to believe she never would. Now that I had been put on an equal footing with everyone else, my feelings had been hurt. With great embarrassment, I realized I had done back to her the same thing by taking away the field trip. She had hurt me and I had wanted to show her that she'd be sorry. I had chosen the one thing within my power that I knew would hurt her back.

Realizing this made me feel worse than ever. What a crass, egotistical boor. I hated myself, hated the world. Feeling absolutely bleak, I could not decide how to recover the situation.

Over our sandwiches at lunch, I unloaded my guilt on Anton. "Boy, I blew it this time," I mumbled into my peanut butter. Why had I ever become a teacher if I had such lousy control over my own feelings? Anton tried to reassure me. She had behaved very badly, he reminded me. She deserved to know that it was unacceptable.

But I felt like a zero. The poor kid. Here this day should have been a happy reunion for everyone. And I came back a shrew. What she had done was not so unpredictable. The kid was upset and was showing it the best way she knew how. Hell, that was why she was in this room to begin with. But what about me? Was that my reason for being there too? This day should have been a joyous affirmation that she could trust me; I returned like I had promised. Instead I yelled at her. And I took away a privilege she didn't even know was in jeopardy. God, how had I ever gotten into teaching?

I spent the entire lunch hour feeling like a monster and not knowing how to fix things. Even if I apologized, I could not undo becoming so mad at her in the morning. I choked unhappily through the last of my sandwich. She had been right. She had never said I could trust her.

Back in the classroom, I sat down next to her. The

other kids were getting ready to go and parents milled around. Sheila sat alone over in the corner.

"Honey, I have to talk to you. I did something wrong this morning. I got mad at you when I was really mad at myself. I told you that you couldn't go on the field trip, but I've changed my mind. You can go. I'm sorry I was angry with you."

Without responding, without even looking at me, Sheila rose and got her coat.

After school, when the other children had gone home, the strained silence between us lingered. I had tried to break it all afternoon, outdoing myself to be funny and make everyone laugh. But Sheila remained apart, holding on to Whitney's hand. I gave up. As in all things, the best healer, I decided, would be time. I was recovering, knowing that I had acted inappropriately, but also knowing, as Anton had pointed out, that I was human.

I took the papers from the basket and sat down to grade them. I had offered to read but Sheila declined and busied herself playing cars on the floor across the room. The first hour passed and Sheila got up to stand by the window and watch the shadows lengthen across the snow. When next I looked up, she was still by the window but she was watching me.

"How come you come back?" she asked softly.

"I just went away to give a speech. I never intended to stay away. This is my job here with you kids."

"But how come you come back?"

"Because I said I would. I like it here."

Slowly she approached the table where I was sitting. The hurt was clear in her eyes now.

"You really didn't think I was coming back, did you?" She shook her head.

Across a tremendous gulf of silence we looked at each other. I could hear the clock jumping the minutes. Onions, the rabbit, rustled in his cage. I was looking at her eyes, wide and fluid and the color of the water where I used to go diving off the coast. I wondered what she was thinking. And I realized sadly, that we never do understand what it is like to be someone else. Nor do we ever seem to be quite able to accept that truth, feeling glibly omniscient despite the limitations of flesh and bone. Especially with children. But we really never know.

She stood twisting an overall strap. "Would you read that book again?"

"Which book is that?"

"The one about the little boy who tamed the fox."

I smiled. "Yeah, I'll read it."

CHAPTER 13

MARCH CAME IN BREEZY AND WARM, A WEL-
come relief for the winter-weary North. The snow finally
melted, and cool, brown mud rose through the grass from
all the water. We were all anxious for spring that year. It
had been a hard winter with more snow and cold than we
usually received.

March was also peaceful as far as school went; as peaceful as one got in a class like mine. There were no vaca-
tions, no disruptions to cause friction, no unexpected
changes. The migrant population was coming up from the
South, the camp swelling to meet their influx. Teachers in
the lounge groused because migrant kids were finding
their way into their classes, but I had nothing to worry
about in that way. The return of the workers, however,
had a strange sad-sweet effect on Anton. When the first
few trucks filled with migrants began arriving, Anton did
not mention it but he became quieter and more distracted.
I finally asked him about it. I was wondering if he were
nostalgic for that less encumbered life-style.

He had smiled when I asked. Smiled and looked at me
in the compassionate way one does when an issue is completely beyond the other's comprehension. Then he drew

up one of the tiny chairs and dropped his huge frame in it. No, he explained to me, he did not miss the migrant lifestyle. There was nothing about living that way for a man to miss. He smiled again, more to himself than to me. What was affecting him, he said, was realizing how much he had changed since the trucks had rumbled out in the autumn. How different from them he had become. How he had never noticed the changing until now. Like Rip van Winkle must have felt upon awaking, he said, then gave a laugh of disbelief. He hadn't even known who Rip van Winkle was last year and now had more in common with Rip than with his own people.

I watched him as he talked. I studied the dark Latin features, the angular bones, the physical stigmata of a hard life too early. We both had changed, in ways I could not quite give words to, but which were no less immense for lack of expression. I was awed that we could have such vast effect on each other's lives and for the most part never realize it, certainly not while it was happening. For several minutes we sat looking at one another, openly, admiringly, the taboo on staring temporarily suspended. So many differences: our backgrounds, our sex, our education, so much. Yet somehow, in some way, we had managed to touch each other. That flicker of understanding silenced the two of us as we sat at the table. There was no need for words.

Like the daffodils, Sheila bloomed in spite of the harsh winter. Each day she was back showing more and more improvement. Within the limits of her situation she was now always quite clean. She would come bounding in each morning, wash her face and brush her teeth. She paid close attention to how she looked, inspecting her image carefully in the mirror. We experimented with new hairstyles. After school some days we played beauty shop. I let her work with my long hair and in turn I was allowed to play with hers, devising new ways to braid or style it. She had become a truly handsome child, evoking comment from the other teachers.

Sarah and Sheila had become fast friends and I caught them sending notes during class occasionally. Sheila had gone home with Sarah to play on several occasions after school before her bus came. And Sheila and Guillermo played together at the migrant camp. Tyler was a bit too much of a priss for Sheila's taste, and she would rebuff Tyler's motherly attentions. I was pleased to see that she generally attracted the favor of the children in the class.

Academically Sheila sailed. She willingly did almost anything I gave her to do. A paper was occasionally destroyed, but only very occasionally. If it happened twice a week, that was the exception. Even at that she had learned to come up and ask for another one. I had her working on third grade reading material and fourth grade math. Both were considerably below her ability level, but because of her deprived background and her fear of failure, I felt it was better to keep her in work which could cement her knowledge and confidence more solidly.

She was still overly sensitive about correction, going off into great sulks or heartrending sighs if she made a mistake. Some days seemed worse than others in that respect and she would spend the whole day with her head buried in her arms in dismal despair over missing one math problem. But as a rule there were not many disasters. With a bit of extra cuddling and reassurance she would usually try again.

Oddly enough in my mind, our falling out over my two days' absence did not appear to have adverse effects on Sheila's emotional stability. For a few days after my return she resorted to hanging on to me again, but soon after, abandoned that behavior. Never again did she do it. We talked a lot about that incident. She seemed to need to rehash the event over and over and over. I had left her. I had come back. She had gotten angry and destructive. I had gotten angry and lost my temper. I had told her I was wrong and I was sorry. Each little piece of the drama she wanted to discuss again and again, telling me how she'd felt, what had made her throw up that day, how she'd been scared. The saga was repeated over and over and over until I thought I would never hear the end of it. It held some secret significance that I did not fully understand and the ritualistic retelling seemed to reassure her. Certainly the fact that I had come back was important, but that was not the only facet she dwelled upon. That we had been angry with each other and weathered that appeared equally significant in her mind. Perhaps she felt assured to have seen me at my worst. She could trust me now, knowing what I was like even when I was upset with her. Whatever it was, she was learning to solve her problems verbally. No longer did she need physical contact; words were enough.

Oddly, the destructiveness all but disappeared after the event of my absence and return. When she became angry, which she still did with great regularity, she did not fly into a rage, throwing things to the floor and rampaging about. Revenge was becoming less important. When I thought about it, I wished I could have fully understood the importance of that incident because in many ways it greatly altered Sheila's behavior. But the full picture always remained a mystery. Sheila still had a lot of problems, but they were becoming more readily solved and much more manageable.

One of the things which still puzzled me was her language. Visiting her father had substantiated that her peculiar speech patterns with the lack of past tense and overuse of "be" did not come from home. As bright as she was, I could not fathom why she persisted in speaking so oddly, although as time passed she did appear to be using more normal speech. During March I decided to finally ask her about it, pointing out that some words were said differently if you were talking about something that happened yesterday. She was surprisingly antagonistic toward my comments, saying that I understood her, didn't I? When I said yes, I did, she asked me what did it matter how she talked if I understood her? That took me off-guard because it made me feel that the behavior was more premeditated than I had previously thought.

No one had any suggestions on the matter. All the speech experts to whom I sent tapes answered saying it was a dialect and often asking if she were black. When I replied that no, she wasn't, and no, it wasn't a family dialect, they had no other ideas. One night Chad and I were discussing it and he suggested that perhaps by not using the past tense, she was trying to keep everything anchored in the present where she could keep better control of things. The more I pondered that, the more possible it seemed. In the end, I concluded it was a psychologically based problem and let it go at that. We did understand what she was saying and perhaps someday she would feel

132

comfortable enough to want to change. Right now, though, she did not.

The issue still uppermost in Sheila's mind was abandonment. She was preoccupied with her mother and her brother, where they were and what they were doing. Often her conversations were punctuated with comments to the effect that if she could have done this thing or that thing better, maybe her family would still be intact. In my mind this was all directly tied to her intense fear of failure.

One night after school Sheila had busied herself doing math problems. She loved math and excelled in it beyond all other areas. From the time she had arrived, she could do basic multiplication and division problems. Together we had worked out the more complicated techniques. She had discovered a dittoed exam from one of the fifth grade classes in a trash can at recess and brought it in to do after school.

When she had finished it, Sheila came over to show it to me. The problems were in division of fractions. This was not an area we had ever covered. Consequently all the problems were wrong because she had not inverted the divisor.

"Here's this. Is it done good?" she asked, handing it to me to look at.

Regarding the paper, I wondered whether or not I should point out the error. "Sheil, I want to show you something." On the back of the paper I drew a circle and divided it into four parts. "Now, if I wanted to know how many eighths were in it . . ." She immediately perceived that the way she was solving the problem would not give the correct answer.

"I done them wrong, didn't I?"

"You didn't know, kiddo. No one showed you."

She flopped down beside me and put her face in her hands. "I wanted to do them right and show you I could do them without help."

"Sheil, it's nothing to get upset about."

She sat for a few moments covering her face. Then slowly her hands slid away and she uncrumpled the paper which she had mashed. "I bet if I could have done math problems good, my Mama, she wouldn't leave me on no

133

highway like she done. If I could have done fifth grade math problems, she'd be proud of me."

"I don't think math problems have anything to do with it, Sheila. We really don't know why your Mama left. She probably had all sorts of troubles of her own."

"She left because she don't love me no more. You don't go leaving kids you love on the highway. And I cut my leg. See?" For the hundredth time the scar was displayed to me. "If I'd been a gooder girl, she wouldn't have done that. She might still love me even now, if I could have been gooder."

"Sheil, we don't really know that. It was a bad thing, but it's over. I don't think your being good or bad had anything to do with it. Your Mama had her own problems to straighten out. I think she loved you a lot; mamas generally do. I think she just couldn't cope with having a little girl right then."

"But she copeded with Jimmie. How come she tooked Jimmie and left me?"

"I don't know, love."

Sheila looked over at me. That haunted, hurt expression was in her eyes. God, I thought, would I never fill that emptiness? Absently she twisted one pigtail. "I miss Jimmie."

"I know you do."

"His birthday's gonna be next week. He be five years old then and I never seen him since he be two. That do be an awful long time." She turned away from me and went to the window, staring out at the winter-wet March afternoon. "I miss Jimmie almost more than anything. I can't forget him."

"I can tell that."

She turned to look at me. "Could we have a birthday party for him? On March twelfth, that be his birthday. Could we have a party like we have for Tyler when it be her birthday in February?"

"I don't think so, kitten."

Her face fell and she shuffled back over to me. "Why not?"

"Because Jimmie isn't here, Sheil. Jimmie lives clear out in California and not here with us."

"It could be just a little birthday party. Maybe just you and me and Anton. Just after school maybe."

I shook my head.

"But I want to."

"I know you do."

"Then why not? Just a little, little party? Please?" Her face had puckered, her voice pleaded. "I'll be your goodest girl. I won't mess up any other math papers."

"That's not the point, Sheila. I'm saying no because Jimmie isn't here anymore. Jimmie's gone. As much as it hurts to think about, Jimmie may not be coming back. I know you miss him a terribly lot, kitten, but I don't think it's a good idea to keep remembering him the way you are. All it does is hurt you."

She covered her face with her hands.

"Sheil, come here and let me hold you." Without removing her hands she came and I lifted her into my lap. "I know you feel awful about this. I can just feel you hurt from sitting here. It's a very hard thing you have to do."

"I miss him." Her voice broke with a dry sob and she clutched at my shirt, shoving her face into my breasts. "I just want him to be here."

"I know you do, love."

"Why did it happen, Torey? Why did she tooked him and leaved me behind? What made me such a bad girl?" The tears shimmered momentarily in her eyes. But as always they never escaped.

"Oh lovey, it wasn't you. Believe me on this. It wasn't your fault. She didn't leave you because you were bad. She just had too many of her own problems. It wasn't your fault."

"My Pa, he says so. He says if I be a gooder girl she'd a never done that."

My heart sank. There was so much to fight and so little to fight with. Why should she believe me and not her father? What could I do to show her he was wrong in that respect? I felt discouraged. "Your Pa made a mistake on this one, Sheil. He doesn't know what happened either and he doesn't know what it's like to be a little girl. He's wrong on this one. Believe me, please, because it's true."

We sat in silence several minutes. I held her close, feeling her warm unsteady breath against my skin. My heart hurt. I could feel it in my chest and it hurt. Her pain soaked through my shirt and my skin and my bones to be absorbed into my heart. God, it hurt.

At last she looked up. "Sometimes, I'm real lonely."
I nodded.

"Will it ever stop?"

Again I nodded, slowly. "Yes. Someday I think it will."
Sheila sighed and pulled away from me, standing up.
"Someday never really ever comes, does it?"

Despite our sad moments, Sheila surprised me by being
filled with joy. She had a tremendous capacity for joy.
Working with these kids whose entire lives were chaotic
tragedies affirmed my faith on a daily basis that humans
are by nature joyous creatures. Sheila's moods fluctuated
a great deal and she was never able entirely to escape the
emotional devastation she had suffered. But by the same
course, she was never far from happiness.

The smallest thing would ignite a merry sparkle in her
eyes and not a day went by now that we did not hear
her skitterish laughter. This was heightened by the fact
that she had been deprived for so long that everything was
new to her. She could not get her fill of the wonders that
the world held. Perhaps her greatest discovery in March
was the flowers.

Our part of the state comes alive in March with cro-
cuses and daffodils waving from every patch of ground.
Sheila was fascinated by the flowers. None had ever
grown in the migrant camp and, as unbelievable as it
seemed to me, she had never before seen a daffodil up
close. One morning I brought a huge bouquet from my
landlady's garden into class.

Sheila came squealing over, toothpaste still in her
mouth. She was just in her T-shirt and underpants, her
bare feet slapping the floor as she ran. "What them things
be?" she gurgled through the toothpaste.

"They're daffodils, silly. You've seen them before,
haven't you?"

Peering at them she shook her head. "Uh-uh. Just in
books, that's all. Them be real flowers?"

"Sure they're real. Touch them."

Putting down her toothbrush, she cautiously reached
out, touching the edge of one flower with her fingertip.
"Oooooh!" she squealed with delight, spraying toothpaste all around. Jumping up and down, she clutched

herself with pleasure. Then stopping suddenly, she hesitantly touched another. Again the little dance of joy.

"Go finish brushing your teeth and get your clothes on, then you can help me put them in a vase."

Dashing back, she spit out the rest of the toothpaste, but was unable to contain her glee long enough to put on the overalls. She came running back. "They do be so soft. Let me touch them."

"Smell them. Daffodils don't smell as good as some flowers, like roses, for instance. But they have a special odor all their own."

She sniffed deeply. "I wanna hug them."

I chuckled. "Flowers don't especially like being hugged."

"But they smell that good and they do be so pretty. They make me feel like hugging them."

"Yes, they do, don't they?" I had gotten out one of the vases a child had made for me years earlier. There were too many flowers to fit in it. Beside me Sheila bounced in delight, first on one foot and then on the other. Her whole body reflected her joy.

"Sheil, would you like a flower of your own?"

She looked up at me, her eyes widening to what seemed to be the very perimeters of her face. "I can have one?"

"Yes, there's too many to fit in my vase. We could put it in a milk carton over by where you always sit at the table."

"Could it really be mine?"

I nodded.

"For me?"

"Yes, silly, for you. Your own flower."

Her face fell suddenly. "My Pa, he wouldn't let me keep it."

I smiled. "Flowers are different than that. They don't last very long, hardly even a day. Your Pa wouldn't care about something like a flower."

Tenderly she reached out and caressed one of the daffodils. "Remember in that book about the fox and the little prince? Remember, the prince had a flower and he tamed it. Remember that?" Her eyes were full of wonder as she looked up at me. "Do you suppose I could tame one? It would be my very own special flower and I could be 'sponsible for it and everything. I could tame it for my very own."

"Well, you'll have to remember flowers don't last too long. But they tame easily. I think you could do it. Which one would you like?" I pointed to the ones left over from the vase.

Considering them all carefully she chose one that looked no different to me from all the others, but it must have said something special. Perhaps the taming had already begun, because like the little prince and his rose, this daffodil was Sheila's and to her it was like no other flower in the world.

Holding the flower gently and stroking its golden cup, she smiled. I had gone over and gotten her overalls and came back, leaning over her, urging her to put her legs in. The other children were arriving, noisy and curious about what was happening. But Sheila stood oblivious, letting me dress her and not looking at the other children. Her lips were pressed tight between her teeth to keep a smile in check.

"My heart do be so big," she whispered, "it be so big and I do reckon I be about the happiest kid for it."

I kissed her soft temple and smiled. Then I picked up the vase of yellow daffodils and took them to the table.

CHAPTER 14

WE LAUGHED A LOT.

Things were not always very funny in our room. Often the things I did find myself laughing about were matters that, if I had stopped and really thought about them, were only tragic. Perhaps the greatest magic of the human spirit is the ability to laugh. At ourselves, at each other, at our sometimes hopeless situation. Laughter normalized our lives.

Whitney, more than anyone else, kept us in line with what was normal. I loved her wholeheartedly for that quality, for never letting me or Anton or the kids ever quite convince her that this room was different.

Despite her shyness, Whitney had a sense of humor that sometimes did not know limits. Her wit could be dry and shockingly adult on occasion, especially when she was alone with Anton and me. However, Whitney was at her best when practical joking. Perhaps I would have been better prepared for that side of her if it had seemed more in keeping with her meek, bumbling exterior. Or maybe if our room had seemed a likelier place for playing practical jokes. Whatever it was, Whitney consistently took me by surprise. I never failed to be genuinely startled by the spring snakes that jumped out of Susannah's crayon box or the fake vomit sitting on the table while Peter and William and Guillermo feigned sudden stomachaches.

When Sheila arrived, that side of Whitney hit its zenith. The other kids loved Whitney's jokes and readily participated in them. Sheila, however, was bright enough to catch on to what Whitney was planning ahead of time, to make creative suggestions of her own, to see the inherent humor in a given situation. And Sheila was naive enough to do some of the crazier things Whitney suggested.

Much of March had passed and nothing happened. That made me suspicious. Each morning I began checking my drawers and my ceramic mug and other things that regularly fell prey to jokes. Usually I could count on Sheila to tip me off, primarily because she could not keep secrets well. Even when she was trying, she was not too sophisticated about hiding the evidence. However, nothing was happening. I did catch the two of them giggling together frequently enough to continue to be on-guard, but as the days went by, nothing occurred. Perhaps this was because Whitney had caught a bad cold and was absent almost a week.

Toward the latter half of the month Mrs. Crum, Freddie's mother, came to visit me after school. A small woman, sparrow-brown and mouse-scared, she slipped inside the door and apologized for bothering me. I had been playing cars on the floor with Sheila and assured her I did not mind being interrupted. Could I help her? Head down, she wrung her hands. So sorry to bother me with her problems. I asked Sheila to trot down to the office and help Anton who was there cutting mimeo stencils. Once we were alone, I invited Mrs. Crum to sit down.

She had come to ask me if the children had been eating anything at school lately. I thought. It was Wednesday, so we had just had cooking. We'd made egg foo young, I told her. Other than that, they hadn't eaten anything. Except lunch, of course. She wrinkled her brow. Freddie had come home three times in the last week and vomited. That would not have surprised her so much, she said, if she could have figured out what it was he was vomiting up. Little bright red, green, blue and yellow balls about a quarter inch in diameter. A couple dozen of them every time.

I was genuinely perplexed. Nothing I could think of fit that description. Not only did we not have any candy because I did not keep candy in the room, but also I did not keep any small nonedibles like that simply because the kids like Freddie or Max or Susannah would put them into their mouths. No, he couldn't be getting them at school, I reassured her. But I promised I would keep an eye on him to be sure.

The next few days went as usual. Whitney was still gone and I got bogged down with end-of-term report cards, so I spent part of the after-school time working while Sheila played by herself. The weekend came and went, then Monday again.

In the afternoon when I came back from taking the other children to their buses, I found Sheila on her knees in front of the cupboard under the sink. She had a colorful assortment of phrases she saved to use when she was especially perturbed. No matter what I did, she persisted in stringing them out when things did not go her way. Now as I came back into the room, I heard her muttering them half-aloud.

"What's wrong, Sheil?"

She leaped to her feet and whirled around. "Nothing."

"What were you swearing about?"

"Nothing."

I came over to the sink. "Didn't sound like nothing to me. What's going on?"

"Someone takeded something that be mine."

"Like what?"

"Just some stuff." She frowned. "I be gonna make an art project out of. I be looking for it and someone stealed it. It ain't in here where I put it."

"Why did you put it there in the first place? You ought to keep your things in your cubby. You know that. Nobody knows what they find under there is yours. What was it anyway?"

"Just some stuff."

"What kind of stuff?"

She shrugged. "Just stuff. That belong to me."

"Well, you go over to the art box. Maybe there are some scraps in there you can use."

About an hour later, there was Mrs. Crum at my door

141

again. Oh so sorry, she began apologizing, but Freddie vomited again. More little colored balls. She had brought some with her this time, all wrapped up in a paper napkin. Despite her timidity, she insisted I look at them and convince her they did not come from my room.

Gritting my teeth I unwrapped the damp napkin. There were eight or ten little not-quite-round spheres in bright, Day-Glo colors. Taking a pencil, I poked at one. It mashed easily to reveal a dark, greenish-brown center. I could not imagine what they were.

Anton, who had been down in the teachers' workroom, came into the room. I beckoned him over.

"Have you seen anything like this around here?" I asked.

He leaned over my shoulder for a closer look. "What the hell?" Taking the pencil from me, he mashed a second one. It, too, crumbled easily.

"Apparently Freddie has been finding them somewhere, eating them and then throwing them up when he comes home from school. Mrs. Crum thinks they're from around here."

"What are they?" Anton asked, skepticism undisguised.

"I haven't the foggiest idea."

Sheila had gotten curious and came over. She tugged at my jeans. "Lemme see."

I pushed her off. "Just a sec."

She went off to drag a chair over and climbed on it to be closer to our height. "Lemme see."

"You know," Anton said, now holding the napkin with its mysterious contents, "this is going to sound dumb, but they look like rabbit turds to me."

"Anton, they're red and green and blue," I replied.

"I know it. But look at the middles. Don't they look like it to you?"

I started to laugh in spite of myself. The ridiculousness of the situation struck me.

Sheila was balancing precariously on a chair beside me, one hand on my arm, one on the collar of my shirt. "Lemme see, Torey."

Anton leaned over toward her and showed the napkin. When she saw the contents of the napkin, she jerked back

142

suddenly, throwing herself off-balance. Both she and the chair fell over.

"You all right?" I asked as she picked herself up.

She nodded. Something about the way she looked at me made me suspicious. Or more precisely, the way she did not look at me.

"Do you know something about this, Sheil? What these little things are?"

Taking a step backwards, she gave a huge shrug.

Anton's eyebrows came down in his I-mean-business look.

"Sheila, did you give something to Freddie he shouldn't have?"

She looked up at us. Innocence written all over her. Big, wide eyes round as china plates. Hair escaped from her ponytail, wispy around her face. She held her lower lip between her teeth and continued to move backwards. For Sheila such innocent demeanor implied guilt.

"Sheila, I want you to tell me about this," I said.

Still no response.

"We know you know," Anton added.

We stared at one another.

"Sheila." My most serious voice. I was having a hard time sounding that way. She looked so damned innocent in the face of such obvious guilt. How she could look that way and betray herself so badly, I did not know.

Finally I approached her, slowly, because fear had creeped into her expression and she still spooked occasionally if someone rushed at her. Putting a hand behind her shoulder, I propelled her back to the table. I kept my fingers on her back and stood behind her so she could not get away again.

"Now suppose you tell us what this stuff is, kiddo. I want to know and I want to know right now."

She stared at the damp napkin full of the colorful little balls which Mrs. Crum had laid on the table. I could feel Sheila pressing back against my hand. I jostled her shoulder.

"I'm losing patience, Sheil. Don't make me angry. These things could hurt Freddie and we need to know what they are. Now tell me."

"Rabbit poop," she said softly.

"Then how come they're all those colors?"

143

"I painted them with temperas."

The situation got the better of Anton and he began to giggle. A hand over his mouth, he smothered the sound.

"For crying out loud, Sheila," I said, "why were you painting rabbit poop?"

"For Whitney."

As I wormed the story out of Sheila, we learned that she and Whitney had been planning to play a joke. For Easter, we were making a large mosaic in the back of the room, which was to be hung in the hallway of the main school building for Parent's Night. It was to be titled "Hopping Down the Bunny Trail." Apparently Whitney had thought it would be funny to substitute the mosaic chips with painted rabbit dung. Sheer adolescent humor. Sheila had been given the ignominious task of wrestling the dung away from Onions, who did not like anyone messing around in his cage for any reason. She was painting it and then drying it under the sink where no one looked much. Freddie must have discovered all this covert activity and assumed the painted dung was candy. Or something. He ate it. From the way Sheila related the whole deal, I gathered that the last week must have been a frustrating one for her. Onions had been uncooperative, Whitney had been absent and Sheila's cache of painted poop kept mysteriously disappearing. No wonder I caught her cursing into the cupboard after school.

Anton could barely contain himself through this recital. Lips tight between his teeth, he rolled his eyes heavenward repeatedly, and coughed into one hand. Mrs. Crum did not see the humor inherent in the whole mess. I might have felt differently too, if it were my son. None of us knew about the toxicity of the substance. I knew the temperas were nontoxic but had no idea about rabbit dung. Anton went to call the poison center. However, since Freddie had been eating them over the last week and had apparently suffered no ill effects, aside from his upset stomach, I was not too worried. Besides, he had been throwing them up unchewed and undigested anyway.

I pointed out the quiet corner to Sheila and suggested she go sit there the rest of the time. She went without protest, but deep, melodramatic sighs were issued so frequently that I was afraid she would hyperventilate. Anton returned with the report from the poison control center and assured Mrs. Crum that no harm would come to Freddie. I apologized to her for the kids' foolishness and escorted her to the door.

Anton and I discussed the situation and decided that we ought to have Whitney come in right then. She lived near the school and I felt it was better to get the matter taken care of when the other children were not around. Although it had been meant as a joke, the affair could have had serious consequences. I preferred to talk it over with Whitney and see how things were.

Anton left to call Whitney. I came over to the quiet chair. Sheila looked up.

"Listen, it's just about time for you to go to your bus. You get your jacket and get started. Anton and I are both too busy to walk you tonight, so you're going to have to take responsibility for yourself. I don't want to hear one single word from anybody that you messed around between here and the bus. Is that clear?"

Sheila nodded.

"Good-bye then. I'll see you tomorrow."

"I do be sorry."

"That's okay. We've talked about it and it's over now."

"You be mad at me?"

"I'll live through it. I know you guys did it as a joke and didn't mean to hurt anybody with it. I understand that. And you know now that it was a kind of dumb thing to do. So we'll just forget it, now that it's over."

She stood up but did not move away from the chair.

"Hurry up or you'll miss your bus."

"You be mad at me?"

"No, Sheil, I'm not mad at you. Now get moving."

"How come you don't smile at me, if you ain't mad?" The worry showed too plainly in her eyes.

Grinning, I came down on my knees to be her height and hugged her against me. I kissed her soundly on the cheek. "You're still a little short on faith, aren't you?" I pushed back her bangs. "Now don't you go home and worry about it, because I'm all done being mad. I wasn't very mad to begin with because what you did wasn't on

145

purpose. Mostly I was just worried about Freddie and when I get really worried, it comes out like I'm mad. But it's all over. Okay? Does that settle it for you?"

She nodded.

"All right. Then scoot or you'll miss that bus."

Whitney was another matter entirely. She arrived with her mother about ten minutes after Sheila left. I had not meant it to become that big a deal. I simply wanted to talk to her. I was not angry. As I had told Sheila, I never really had been. Mostly, I had been worried and also a little embarrassed in front of Mrs. Crum. Yet there had been potential danger in the situation and I felt Whitney needed to be aware of that. However, Whitney's mother made a federal case of the deal.

Anton had had to talk to her on the phone and had explained a little bit of the problem. She came storming into the school, hauling Whitney by the arm as if she were a little girl. A tall woman with starched blond hair, Whitney's mother marched into my room and demanded I tell her what happened. I explained best as I could. At that she turned to Whitney with an anger I could not have managed if Freddie had died from the stuff.

"Mrs. Blake? Mrs. Blake?" I kept trying to interrupt. "If I could just talk . . . Mrs. Blake?"

Anton was in the middle of the fray too, trying to distract her. "Would you like a cup of coffee, Mrs. Blake?"

All the time Whitney sat in one of the little chairs and sobbed.

I don't remember how we shut her mother up. We did finally, and Anton took her down to the lounge for coffee. I figured that was a just reward for her. By that time of day, the coffee would have been in the pot for over eight hours.

Whitney and I were alone. I was embarrassed to be there, to have heard her mother talk to her like that. She must have felt humiliated. I was embarrassed to the point that I did not know what to say. Bringing over a box of tissues, I set them on the table in front of her. I hesitated momentarily, wondering if I should apologize or something. I mumbled something about giving her a few minutes to collect herself while I sorted out the kids' papers and put them in their cubbies for the next morning.

146

When I came back, I sat down beside her and put an arm around her shoulder. Whitney turned and clutched me. The move had been unexpected and my chair wobbled with her weight against me but I closed my arms around her; she was so hungry for comforting.

"Listen, things aren't this bad, Whitney." I smoothed her hair back from her face. "Anton and I, we're not that mad at you. I'm not that mad at all."

She straightened up in her chair and took an umpteenth Kleenex. "I was just joking."

"I know you were. And I'm not mad. I didn't mean to get you in all this trouble. Believe me, I wouldn't have had you come over if I'd known it would be this bad for you."

"Oh, my mom gets mad at anything."

"Yeah, well, it wasn't that big a deal. I just wanted you to know that you have to be a little careful around here. These aren't normal kids, Whitney. You have to watch things so much more around them."

She nodded and wiped at more tears.

"Kids like Freddie don't know what's edible and what isn't. And Sheila's too little to know she shouldn't be doing that sort of thing."

"I didn't think anybody would get hurt. I didn't mean this to happen."

"Oh, sweetheart, I know that. And this time, nobody did get hurt. We just came awfully close. It was only a silly thing you did without thinking. I love your sense of humor, Whitney, and I love the way you show the kids how to laugh. But these are special kids. We need to take extra good care of them."

She braced her head in her hands and stared at the tabletop. "I never do anything right. I screw up everything I do."

"It just seems that way right now. But you know that isn't true."

"My mom's going to kill me."

"This isn't any of your mom's worry. It's just yours and mine. Anton will take care of your mom and if he doesn't, I'll talk to her."

"I am sorry, Torey."

"Yeah, I know you are."

"What's going to happen to me?"

147

"Nothing."

Whitney would not look at me; she continued to stare at the table. I had a hand on her shoulder still and could feel the warmth through her shirt. We sat a long, long time in silence.

"Can I tell you something, Torey?"

"Yeah."

Still no way she could look at me. "This is about the only place in the world I like to be. Everybody teases me about it. All the time. They say: Why do you want to hang around with a bunch of crazy people all the time? They think I'm crazy too. You know, not nice crazy, but really mental. Because otherwise why would I want to be here so much?"

"Well," I replied, "then they must think the same thing about Anton and me. We must be crazy too."

"Do people ever say that to you?" For the first time she looked at me.

"Not to me. But I suspect there are more than a few who think it."

"Why are you here?"

I smiled. "I guess because I like very honest relationships. So far the only people whom I've found to be that honest are either children or crazy. So this place seems to be a natural for me."

Whitney nodded. "Yes, I guess that's what I like too—the way everybody shows exactly what they feel. So at least if someone hates you, you know it." She smiled wanly. "The funny thing is, these kids don't seem as crazy to me sometimes as normal people do. I mean . . ." her voice trailed off.

I nodded. "Yes, I know what you mean."

Chad was waiting for me when I arrived home, none too patiently. He had brought over a couple of cartons of moo goo gai pan from Jeno's Chinese Take-Out.

"Where on earth have you been? It's practically seven o'clock." He had been trying to keep the food warm by setting cartons and all in a frying pan. The kitchen smelled of scorched paper.

"At school."

"This late? Jesus, I've been here practically an hour. What were you doing?"

"Well, one of my kids had been vomiting up these little colored balls at home and his mom was suspicious that it was something he got into at school. So she brought this soggy napkin full of what he'd been throwing up."

Chad began to giggle. He had turned away from me to jiggle the frying pan with the cartons in it. I could see his shoulders shake.

"So Anton and I began dissecting these little balls and they turned out to be rabbit turds."

Chad's giggles became full laughter. And contagious. I began to chuckle.

"Anyway, Sheila had been getting the turds out of Onions' cage and painting them with temperas. God only knows when she was doing it, but evidently Freddie found them and was eating them. I guess he thought they were candy or something."

Both of us were laughing. I could hardly get the last words out. The smell of scorching cartons wafted up between us but by that time the tears were rolling down our cheeks. My side hurt. And still we laughed.

"I'm sorry I asked," Chad finally gasped.

"I'm not," I replied.

CHAPTER 15

THE CALL THAT I HAD BEEN DREADING CAME the third week in March. Ed Somers' low, rumbling voice came over the telephone. When the secretary had called my room that evening after school to tell me I had a phone call, I had a premonition this was the one. When I heard Ed's voice I knew, even before he said it.

"Torey, the director called today. They have an opening at the state hospital."

My pulse began to race when I heard him say that. The beating was so hard in my ears that I could not hear easily. "Ed, she doesn't have to go, does she?"

"Tor, I told you this was only a temporary placement. The court ordered that she be placed in the state hospital when an opening came up. It really is out of our hands. Your placement was only temporary."

"But she's changed so much. She's not the same child. Ed, she won't make it in the hospital."

"Listen, it was all settled before either of us got into it. You know that, we discussed it before. Besides, it'll be in her best interest. Look at that terrible home situation she has. She hasn't got a chance in hell to make it anyway, Tor. You know that. Christ, you work every day with

150

these kids. You, of all people, should know when a kid's got too much stacked against her."

"But she hasn't, Ed," I cried. "This kid has so much. She could make it. She can't go into the hospital now."

Ed could be heard making clucking noises on his side of the phone. There was a long silence as he lit a cigarette. "Tor, you've done a hell of a good job with those kids. I honestly don't know how you do it sometimes. But you've gone too far with this one. You've gotten too involved. I could tell that back with that incident in January. This kid's case was decided long before she ever reached us."

"Then undecide it."

"It's out of my hands. After that burning incident, the state committed her. To placate the boy's parents, that was the only alternative."

"Ed, this is ludicrous. God Almighty, the child is six years old. This can't happen."

"I know how you're feeling, Torey, I really do. I'm awfully sorry this is having to happen this way because I know you've gotten involved with the girl. But she's a court case. We both knew how it would turn out. And I am sorry."

I went down to the teachers' lounge, unable to go back to my room where Sheila was playing. I sat and drank coffee, which I normally never touch, all the while trying to keep the tears back. Ed was right. I had gotten too involved; she mattered too much to me. I could not verbalize my frustration; I was not finding the right words. The chattering over lesson plans and art projects and the school carnival got to me. Finally I ended up going back to my room to get away from the lounge-dwellers who were so filled with after-school merriment.

When Anton saw me, he did not ask what had happened—he knew. He motioned Sheila over to the table where he was setting up a project for the next day and asked her to help him. I stood in the doorway looking around the room. Not a very remarkable place by the looks of it, I thought. Too long and narrow, too dark, too crowded with animal cages that smelled and pillows that lost all their stuffing on the carpet. Not even room for a teacher's desk. I could have used a teacher's desk right then; something to go and hide behind; something that shouted, "LEAVE ME ALONE," without my saying it.

151

But there was none. Wearily, I went over to the pillows behind the animal cages and sank down onto them.

Within seconds Sheila was standing before me, her eyes scrutinizing my face. "You ain't happy," she stated quietly. She had her hands stuffed into the pockets of her overalls. How much she had grown, I thought. There must have been two inches between the overalls and her shoes. Or perhaps there always had been and I hadn't noticed.

"No, I'm not happy."

"How come?"

"Sheila, come over here," Anton called. Sheila remained motionless, her eyes piercing mine, probing my mind. I was wondering if I really had gotten too involved. She was such a beautiful child to me. To be sure, an ordinary passerby would have thought she looked like any of a hundred thousand other children. But she alone was more important to me than all the rest of them together. I loved her, although I certainly hadn't intended to. And loving her had made her so important to me. Now I was " 'sponsible." I could feel the tears in my eyes.

Sheila knelt beside me, the worry rippling across her face. "How come you cry?"

"I'm not very happy."

Anton came over and lifted Sheila to her feet. "Come on, tiger, you come help me put away papers."

"Uh-uh," Sheila twisted out of his grasp, moving out of reach.

I waved a hand at him. "That's okay, Anton. I'm all right." He nodded and left us.

For a long moment Sheila regarded me, her eyes flooded with concern. The tears remained unfallen in my own but I could not make them go away. Nor could I bring myself to look at her. I was embarrassed to show such shaky composure and I was worried about frightening her.

But she stood apart watching me. Then slowly she came over and sat beside me. Touching my hand tentatively, she spoke. "Maybe if I hold your hand, you'll feel better. Sometimes that helps me."

I smiled at her. "You know, kid, I love you. Don't ever forget that. If the time ever comes and you're alone or scared or anything else bad ever happens, don't forget I love you. Because I do. That's really all one person can do for another."

Her brow wrinkled. She did not understand what I was saying. I suppose I knew she wouldn't because she was so young. But I had to say it. I had to know, for my own peace of mind, that I had told her I had done my best.

I rolled over on the bed to look at Chad. We had been watching TV all evening and not talking. I was too preoccupied to concentrate on conversation. At first I had not even told him the particulars of what had happened; but as the evening wore on, my mind was coming out of the first haze of shock and beginning to tick again.

"Chad?"

He looked in my direction.

"Is there a legal way to contest what they plan to do with Sheila?"

"What do you mean?"

"Well, you know. Is there a legal way to fight the commitment? I mean could someone like me do it? Someone who isn't her guardian?"

"*You* fight it?"

"Someone has to. I think the school district would back me. Maybe."

"I suppose you could try."

I frowned. "My problem is that I can't figure out where to start. To whom do we appeal? The courts committed her and you can't take a court to court, can you? I don't have any idea how to go about this."

"I imagine you'd have to call a hearing with her father and the parents of the little boy she abused and the child protection workers and all that. You could go through due process. You know all that."

I did not know. I had about as much understanding of the judicial system as I did the theory of relativity. But I hated Chad to think so. "Would you take it on, Chad?"

His eyebrows shot up. "Me?"

I nodded.

"I don't know anything about that kind of thing. What you need is someone specializing in that sort of law. Cripes, Tor, my experience is confined to getting the drunks out of jail."

I smiled. "Your experience and my bank account are

153

about equal. I'm supposing that if I advocate, I'll have to pay for it."

Chad rolled his eyes. "Another charity case, huh?" He grinned. "I guess no one ever promised me I'd get rich."

"Oh, someday you will. Just not this year."

When the superintendent of school discovered that I had engaged a lawyer to look into the case, there was a meeting scheduled immediately. For the first time I met Mrs. Barthuly, Sheila's former teacher, face-to-face. She was a petite woman in her early forties with a delicate smile. As all five-foot-nine-inches of me in my Levi's and tennis shoes towered over her, I could well imagine Sheila might have been a trial to her. She wore an Anne Klein scarf and platform shoes and looked like a model for a Chanel No. 5 advertisement on television. Smelly, earthy-minded Sheila must have been hard to contend with.

Ed Somers was also there, as well as Allan, the psychologist, Mr. Collins, Anton, the superintendent and the resource room teacher who had had Sheila in kindergarten the year before. In the beginning it was not a particularly comfortable meeting for me. Not knowing my relationship with Chad, the superintendent felt that I had overstepped my boundaries in consulting a lawyer on this case without going through him. Perhaps he was right. I explained that I had discussed the matter with Ed and he felt there was no way we could touch the case, so I had simply checked into the legal recourse available.

Despite our touchy start, once the meeting got underway, a transition took place. I had brought along examples of Sheila's schoolwork and some videotapes that Anton had made of her in class. Allan reported on the test results. Sheila's former teachers were impressed and said so. Even Mr. Collins, whom I feared would be angry about this next example in a long history of my impulsive acts, commented on the overall improvement in Sheila's behavior. Unexpectedly, I felt a rash of affection toward him as he spoke.

The superintendent was less enthusiastic, saying that this really wasn't our matter because of the abuse incident. Yet he was encouraged by Sheila's progress and by her unusual IQ. He cautiously agreed to stand behind me in stating that the state hospital was not the most appropriate placement for Sheila and that he thought she could be maintained in the public school system without endangering the other students. He asked that Chad come in and see him. Despite the superintendent's attempt to keep the mood of the meeting low-key, I left in jubilant spirits.

The other major person to involve was Sheila's father. Anton went on scouting duty. The next time he saw the man home, Anton called me, and Chad and I came out immediately.

As the time before, Sheila's father had been drinking. He had had a bit more this second time and was a little jollier.

"Sheila doesn't belong in the state hospital," I explained. "She's doing very nice work in school and I think she might even be able to go back to a regular class next fall."

He tipped his head slightly. "Why do you care what they want to do with her?"

The question echoed in my head, a repeat of what Sheila so often asked me. Why *did* I care? "You've got a special daughter," I replied. "Going to the state hospital would be the wrong move for her. I don't want to see that happen to her because I think she can lead a normal life."

"She's crazy as a loon, that girl is. They told you what she done, didn't they? She damn near burned that little kid to death."

"She doesn't need to be crazy. She's not. Even now, she's not crazy. But she will be if she goes down there. It'd get worse in the long run. You don't want your daughter down in the state hospital."

He heaved a great sigh. He did not understand me. All his life people had been after him. Things had always gone wrong. He'd been in trouble, Sheila had been in trouble. He had learned to trust nobody. And so had his daughter. In their world it was safer that way. Now I came and he could not understand.

We talked far into the night. Chad and Anton drank beer with him while I made notes. Sheila, who was keeping her usual vigil on us from the far corner, fell asleep on the floor while we talked. I did not know if she understood why I was there and what was going on. I had not told her anything specific because I did not want to frighten her needlessly, nor did I want to give her false hopes.

But after that night I suspected she would know. It would be better in the end, I supposed.

Her father agreed with us eventually. At last we convinced him that it was not "charity" or "do-gooding" or a nasty trick. He began to perceive the real reasons, which I had trusted he would if we persisted long enough. I had trusted that he did have some paternal instinct under that crust. In his own way, he loved Sheila and needed as much compassion as she did.

That was a strange evening. All of us were a little tipsy. Chad with his experience of defending the skid-row residents seemed to get along with Sheila's father better than the rest of us. He and her father would slap each other's backs in boozy camaraderie when I tried to get the conversation back onto the track and then they'd ply Anton and me with another can of beer. In a way, I was glad the hospital situation came up. It forced us to recognize each other's places in Sheila's life; that was better for everybody.

The hearing was held on the very last day of March. It was a dark, cold, windy day, promising snow on the eve of April. Not a good day to boost spirits. I had to take the afternoon off from school as did Anton. Mr. Collins came with us too. Surprisingly, in my opinion, he was very supportive of me, coming into my room in the morning and talking in a warm, fatherly way. Of all the people I had encountered, I would have least expected this change in him, because I had nursed a childish one-dimensional picture of him since the incident in Mrs. Holmes' room. At first I was suspicious of him, wondering what prompted this change, if he were simply protecting his own interests. But as I aired out some of the closed portions of my own mind I came to see that he cared in his own way as much for the children as I. Even for Sheila.

It was a closed hearing. Across the room from us were the parents of the little boy and their lawyer. Milling about were a multitude of state and county people. With us were Anton, Allan, Mrs. Barthuly, Ed, and the superintendent. Sheila's father arrived late, but he did come finally and he was sober. My heart ached seeing him. He had on a suit that must have been a reject from Goodwill. The seams were frayed, the jacket stained and worn, the pants mended. His huge belly pulled the jacket tight and made it gape, straining on the buttons. Obviously, though, he had tried to look nice. His face was freshly shaven and he reeked of dime-store after-shave.

Outside the courtroom on a hard oak bench sat Sheila. Chad felt it would be best if she could be there. He thought perhaps he might need her if things did not go smoothly.

Sheila had come dressed in her overalls and T-shirt. I had so wished we could have dressed her nicely, but time had run out. So over the lunch hour I had given her a very thorough bath in the sink and brushed her hair until it was neat and shiny. If nothing else, she was clean. She had to sit alone outside the courtroom so we had brought a number of books to entertain her. However, when the judge found out that the child in question was being left unattended, he sent a court clerk out to sit with her.

The hearing went much differently from what I had expected. I had never been in a court before and all my information came from television. But this was not like TV. The lawyers spoke quietly and each of us presented our material. I had brought along the videotapes to illustrate Sheila's growth in my classroom in the three months she had been with us. Allan reiterated his findings from the tests. Ed spoke of the possible programs for her in the public schools should she continue to need special services after my class.

Then the parents of the little boy were questioned about the incident in November. Sheila's father was asked about how carefully he watched his daughter and if, in his opinion, she had seemed to improve in the last months. It was a very quiet hearing. No one raised a voice. No one even appeared emotionally involved. It was so different from what I had expected.

Then we were all asked to leave the courtroom while the lawyers and the judge finished up the case. I was so proud of Chad. Despite our long, enduring relationship, I had never seen him work professionally. Now in front of me I saw a different man from the one I knew lounging on the bed in front of the TV. He seemed so sure of himself, so at ease in the court surroundings. I was so proud of him for taking on the hassle of a case he knew would never earn him any money and for taking my bewildered queries and turning them into a real chance to keep Sheila with us.

Down the hallway the boy's parents sat. The strain showed on their faces. Mouths pulled tight and grim. Eyes staring without seeing. I wondered what they were thinking. I could not tell from their faces. Did they have the compassion to forgive Sheila for what she had done? Or were their hearts still too burdened with grief and with fear? Were they still nursing in deep, unspeakable recesses the hope that her life would be as crippled as they feared she had made their son's? I could not tell from looking at them.

The father turned his head and met my eyes briefly. Both of us looked away. They were not bad people. Not the kind I could work up a hate for. When they had testified, their voices had been soft without detectable anger. If anything, they spoke sadly. Unhappy to have the issue reopened. To be in court a second time. To have their lives once more disrupted by this child. In a way I wished I could have hated them; it would have made the decision either way easier for me to accept. But I could not. They had only done what they thought best. Their fault, if anything, was nothing more than ignorance of mental illness. And fear. Now a judge, a man who did not know either of us, nor either of the children, would be the one to decide—on an issue that had no black or white. I wondered how they felt. I wished I had the courage to get up and go to them and ask. I wished there were a way it could be different.

Sheila was sitting on my lap. She had been drawing a picture when we had come out and was now trying to tell me about it. My self-absorption was annoying her. She put a hand up and physically moved my head to look at her. "Look at my picture, Tor. It be a picture of Susannah Joy. See, she gots on that dress she wears to school so much."

I looked down. Sheila had long been envious of Susannah Joy. Susie was the only child in our classroom to come from an affluent family. She was always immaculately dressed and had a splendid wardrobe of frilly little frocks. Sheila was inelegantly envious. She longed for a dress, just one dress like Susannah had. Day after day, she would page through catalogues and pick out dresses she would like to have. Time and again would come entries on the subject into her journal. Only the week before I had found in the correction basket Sheila's creative writing paper.

I do my best writing for you Torey from now on I do be a gooder girl and do my best work I promise. I want to tell you what I do last night. I go down and wait for my father he be at the opptomrix who fistes eye glasses. So I got to walk around for a while and I look in them windows sometimes. Some times I wish I could by the things in them windows. Some times they be so prety. I seen a dress that be red and blue and be white too and it gots lace on it and be long and beautiful. I ain't never had a dress like that and it was prety torey. I sort of wish I could have it. It be my size to I think. I ask my pa if I could by it but he sad "no". That be too bad cos it be so nice and I aint never had a real dress. And I could a wored it to school like Susannah Joy do. She gots lots of dresses. But I couldnt so we went home and my pa he by me some M&Ms instead and toled me "to go to bed Sheila" so I did.

That little essay had hurt me in a funny, unidentifiable way. It seemed one of the saddest things she had ever written. But Sheila went on, knowing she could not have a dress, accepting it and continuing to dream.

Sheila prattled on about the picture she was holding, showing me intricacies in the drawing. Yet she noticed my mind was wandering. She hadn't been called in, which I took as a good sign, but she was aware of the tension among us.

Then at last the doors to the judge's chambers opened. From the minute I saw Chad's face, I knew what the ruling had been. He stopped about eight feet from us, a crisp smile tight on his face. Then he grinned. "We won."

Noise erupted in the hallway and we danced about hugging one another. "We won! We won! We won!" Sheila shrieked, bouncing midst everyone's legs. We all laughed at her jubilance although I doubted she knew the impact of what she was saying.

"I think this calls for a celebration, don't you?" Chad

asked. He was pulling on his trench coat. "What do you say we go down to Shakey's and order the biggest pizza they have?"

The others were beginning to leave. I glanced briefly down the hallway toward the boy's parents, who were putting on their coats. Once again I wished I had the courage to walk those twenty feet down the corridor and speak to them. Chad was talking to me about pizza, Sheila was jumping around my legs, scrabbling at my belt to be acknowledged, school people were yelling good-byes.

"Well, what do you say?" Chad asked again. "You want to go or are you going to stand there all evening?" He gave me a playful nudge.

I turned back to him and nodded.

"What about you?" Chad said to Sheila. "You want to come with Torey and me to get pizza?"

Her eyes widened and she nodded. I bent down and picked her up to bring her up to our level of the conversation.

Apart from us stood Sheila's father. Alone. His hands stuffed into the pockets of his ill-fitting suit. He stared at the floor. He seemed lonely to me, lonely and forgotten. This had not been his battle we had just won and it was not to him Sheila had gone. She had waited with us in the hallway and now she celebrated with us. It was our victory. He had not been a part of it. Courts had only been bad places for him in the past; they were frightening places. In his tattered suit and cheap after-shave lotion, he made a strange and striking contrast to the school district and government people. I realized with great sadness that even his daughter was not his own. She was one of us; he was not.

Chad must have perceived the same loneliness I did. "Do you want to join us?"

For a moment I thought I saw a flicker of pleasure on his face. But he shook his head. "No, I have to be going."

"It is all right if Sheila comes with us, isn't it?" Chad asked. "We'll bring her home later."

He nodded, a soft smile on his lips as he regarded his daughter. She was still in my arms, still wiggling with excitement, mindless of her father.

"You're sure you won't come with us?"

"No."

For a long moment we looked at each other, the universe between us never bridging. Then Chad reached into his pocket and took out his wallet. Pulling out a twenty-dollar bill, he handed it to Sheila's father. "Here. Here's your share of the fun."

He hesitated and I did not think he would accept it, knowing his disdain for charity. But uncertainly he extended his hand and took the bill. He mumbled a thank you, then he turned and walked away down the long corridor.

Sheila, Chad and I all piled into Chad's little foreign car and sped off to the pizza parlor. "Hey, Sheila, what kind of pizza do you like?" Chad asked over his shoulder to Sheila in the back seat.

"I don't know. I ain't never had no pizza."

"Never had pizza?" Chad exclaimed. "Well, we might have to do this more often, huh?"

If she never had pizza before, one would never have known it from Sheila's behavior. Her eyes were wide and shiny when the pizza arrived and she grabbed for it like a pro. Chad ordered the biggest, fullest-topped pizza he could find on the menu as well as a pitcher of soda pop. It was a magical moment. Sheila was alive and animated, talking constantly. She was intrigued by Chad and ended up sitting on his lap while we listened to the piano player entertain us. Chad commented that he had never seen a little kid eat so much food in one sitting in his life. Teasingly, Sheila told him she could eat at least a hundred pizzas if he had money to buy them and burped loudly to prove it.

Except for having seen her briefly the night we had gone to visit her father, Chad had never met Sheila. Early in the evening it was clear he thought she was one special person. Obviously the feeling was mutual. They laughed and kidded each other throughout the stay at the pizza place.

Night had fallen and the evening crowd was beginning to drift in. We had eaten the entire gigantic pizza, plus the pop, plus a round of soft ice cream. We had listened to the piano player so long that he coaxed Chad up to play "Heart and Soul" with him. But it was apparent that Chad and Sheila were not ready to part company.

Chad leaned way over the table to look at Sheila. "What's the thing you'd like best in the world, if you could have it?" he asked. My heart flinched because I knew Sheila would answer that she wanted her Mama and Jimmie back and that would dampen our mood.

Sheila pondered the question a long moment. "Real or pretend?"

"Real."

Again she sat pensively. "A dress, I think."

"What kind of dress?"

"Like Susannah Joy gots. One that gots lace on it."

"You mean all you'd want in the whole world is just a dress?" Chad's eyes wandered above Sheila's head to me.

Sheila nodded. "I ain't never had a dress before. Once a lady from a church bringed us out some clothes and there be this dress in it. But my Pa, he don't even let me try it on. He says we don't 'cept no charity from no one." She frowned. "I didn't think it would hurt just to try it on, but my Pa, he said I'd get a pounding if I did, so I didn't."

Chad looked at his watch. "It's almost seven o'clock. I don't think the stores in the Mall close until nine." He looked from me to Sheila. "What if I told you this is your lucky day?"

Sheila regarded him quizzically. She still did not know what was going on. "What do you mean?"

"What if I told you that in a few minutes we were going out to the car and go buy you a dress? Any dress you want."

Sheila's eyes got so big I thought they would break her face. Her mouth dropped and she looked at me. Then suddenly she was crestfallen. "My Pa, he wouldn't let me keep it."

"I think he would. We'll just tell him that's your share of the fun. I'll go in with you when we take you home. I'll tell him."

Sheila was beside herself. She leaped from her chair and danced in the aisle, colliding with unsuspecting patrons. She hugged me. She hugged Chad. Surely she would have exploded then and there if we hadn't left.

The next hour was a giddy one. We walked the aisles

162

of the two big department stores in the Mall, Sheila holding on to our hands and swinging between us. Once we found the little girls' dresses, she turned unexpectedly shy and would not even look at them, instead shoving her face into my leg. Dreams close up can be quite hard to handle.

Finally I selected a few that were pretty and had lace and I dragged Sheila into a fitting room to try them on. Once we were alone she came back to life. Stripping off the overalls and shirt until she stood naked except for her underpants, Sheila lifted the dresses up to inspect them carefully. She was such a scrawny little thing with a sway back and a little kid's fat stomach that only emphasized her skinniness. Now alone with the dresses she became too excited to try them on and danced around the small room in circles. I captured her around the waist and shoved her into one dress. What a magic moment. Sheila preened herself in front of the three-way mirror and then ran out to show Chad. We must have spent a half hour closeted in that little room while Sheila tried to decide among three dresses. She tried each of them on at least four times. At last she chose one, a red-and-white dress with lace at the neck and around the sleeves.

"I'm gonna wear it every day to school," she said enthusiastically.

"You look so pretty."

She was watching me in the mirror. "Can I wear it home?"

"If you want."

"I do!" Her sudden smile faded and she turned to me. She climbed onto my lap, touching my face softly with one hand. "You know what I wish?"

"That you could have all three dresses?"

She shook her head. "I wish you was my Mama and Chad was my Daddy."

I smiled.

"It almost seems that way now don't it? Tonight, I mean. It almost seems like you are really my folks, huh?"

"We're something better than that, Sheil. We're friends. Friends are better than parents, because it means we love each other because we want to, not because we have to. We choose to be friends."

She looked at me for a long time, sitting on my knees

and gazing into my eyes. Finally she sighed and slid off. "I wish we could be both. We could be family and friends both."

"Yes, that would be nice."

Her forehead wrinkled. "Could we just pretend?" she asked tentatively. "Just for tonight, could we pretend? Pretend that you and Chad was my folks and you was bringing your little girl out to buy her a dress? Even though she gots lots of dresses at home, you was bringing her out to buy another 'cause she wanted it and you loved her a lot?"

All my psychology class training urged me to say no. But as I saw her eyes, my heart wouldn't let me. "I suppose just for tonight we could pretend. But you have to remember it's just pretend and just for tonight."

She leaped up in a great bounce and tore out of the dressing room, still in her underwear. "I'm gonna tell Chad!"

Chad was amused to find out that while we were in the fitting room he had become a father. He played the part to the hilt. It was a mystical night filled with a lot of unspoken magic for all three of us. Sheila fell asleep in my arms on the way out to the migrant camp and after Chad parked the car, I woke her.

"Well, Cinderella," Chad said opening the door, "it's time to go home."

She smiled at him sleepily.

"Come on, I'll carry you in and tell your Daddy what we've been up to."

She hesitated a moment. "I don't wanna go," she said softly.

"It's been a nice night, hasn't it?" I replied.

She nodded. A silence fell between us. "Can I kiss you?"

"Yes, I think so." I enveloped her in a tight hug and kissed her. I felt her soft lips touch my cheek. And she kissed Chad as he lifted her out of my lap and carried her into her house.

We drove home in silence. Pulling up in front of my place we sat in the car, not speaking. Finally Chad turned to me, his eyes shining in the wan glow of the streetlight. "She's a hell of a little kid."

164

I nodded.

"You know," he said, "it probably sounds dumb to say, but I pretended right along with her tonight. I wished we were a family too. It seemed so easy. And so right."

I smiled into the darkness, feeling a comfortable quiet drift down around us.

CHAPTER 16

APRIL CAME IN WITH A SNOWSTORM. AL-though everyone bemoaned this parting shot of winter, it was one of those deep white fluffy snowfalls that are so lovely to look at. However, it stalled everything with its fierce depth, so school was suspended for two days.

When we returned, Sheila announced during the morning discussion that her Uncle Jerry had come to live with them. He had been in jail according to Sheila, although she couldn't remember what for, and now he was out looking for a job. She seemed quite excited about this new member of her family, telling us how Uncle Jerry had played with her all day during the snowstorm when she was bored.

We quickly returned to our routine. There was a trace of euphoria remaining from our victory in court. Although the children were not aware of what had happened, both Anton and I remained in high spirits. And if we were happy, Sheila in her new dress was positively radiant. Every day she wore the red-and-white dress, parading in front of the other kids in an obvious attempt to evoke the same kind of jealousy that Susannah had so successfully caused in her. She told them how on her "trial day"

166

she won and got to go to dinner with Chad and me and got her prized dress. Before long, everyone wanted a trial and I had to ask Sheila not to dwell on it. But while her speech with the other children lessened on the topic, with me after school it was the only topic. Like our incident in February over my absence, this had to be gone over repetitively, in minute detail: we had gone to Shakey's, we had had a tremendous pizza, Sheila had eaten lots and lots. Then we went to buy the dress and pretended we were a real family. Over and over and over she would recount the details, her face animated with memory. I let her go on about it because there seemed to be something therapeutic for her in it, just as in the February incident. Interestingly enough, Jimmie had been all but forgotten. I did not hear his name mentioned for days on end. That had been an evening of sheer, unspoiled happiness for Sheila and she didn't seem able to savor it completely enough. But then I suppose when those moments are far and few between, they are even rarer treasures. So I patiently listened, again and again and again.

One morning almost halfway into April Sheila arrived at school subdued. Anton had gone to meet her at the bus, but the bus had been late and she came in after morning discussion had started. She was wearing her old overalls and T-shirt again and was pale. Sitting down on the outer fringe of the group, she listened but did not participate.

Twice during the half-hour session she got up and went into the bathroom. I worried that she might be ill because she looked so pale and seemed so restrained. But the others were clamoring for attention and my mind was distracted.

When I was handing out math assignments I could not find Sheila, only to discover that she was in the bathroom again. "Don't you feel well today, hon?"

"I'm okay," she replied, taking the math papers from me and going over to her place at the table. I watched her as she went. She was speaking more now, using the proper verbs and I was pleased.

Late in the hour, just before freetime, I came over and sat down with Sheila to show her how to do a group of new math problems. I took her on my lap. Her body was surprisingly rigid as I held her. I felt her forehead to see if

167

she were hot. But she wasn't. Yet she was certainly acting oddly. "Is something wrong, Sheil?"

She shook her head.

"You're all tense."

"I'm okay," she reasserted, and returned to the math problems.

As the lesson concluded, I lifted her off from my lap to the floor. On the leg of my jeans was a widening red spot. I stared at it not fully comprehending what it was. Blood? I looked at Sheila. "What on earth is going on?"

She shook her head, her face emotionless.

"Sheila, you're bleeding!" Down the inside of her right pants leg spread a red stain. Picking her up I rushed into the bathroom and shut the door behind us. Unbuckling the overall straps, I let them fall around her ankles. Blood had stained her underpants and ran down both legs. Wadded into her underwear were paper towels. Apparently that had accounted for the numerous trips to the bathroom earlier. She had been trying to staunch the blood flow so that it would not come through and show.

"Good God, Sheila, *what* is going on?" I cried, my voice sounding louder and more alarmed than I had meant it to. Fear rose in me as I pulled away the last of the towels from her clothing. Bright red blood trickled from her vagina.

But Sheila stood immutable. No emotion ran across her face. Her eyes were blank, looking at but not seeing me. She was paler than I had thought out in the dimmer classroom light; God, she was white. I wondered how much blood she had lost. In an attempt to wake her out of her stoicism, I grabbed her shoulders and shook her. "Sheila, what happened? You have to tell me. You can't play games now. What happened to you?"

She blinked like one coming out of a heavy sleep. She was paying a great price to cut off the pain and the emotion. "Unca Jerry," she began softly, "he tried to put his pecker in me this morning. But it wouldn't fit. So he tooked a knife. He said I was keeping him out, so he put the knife inside me to make me stop."

I went numb. "He put a knife in your vagina?"

She nodded. "One of the silverware knives. He said I'd be sorry for not letting him put his pecker in me. He said this'd hurt a whole lot more and I'd be sorry."

"Oh God, Sheila, why didn't you tell me? Why didn't you let me know?" Fearful that she had already lost too much blood, I wrapped a towel around her and picked her up.

"I's scared to. Unca Jerry told me not to tell. He said he'd do it again if I told on him. He said worser thing would happen if I told."

Rushing out of the bathroom carrying Sheila, I told Anton to watch the class. I grabbed my car keys and raced toward the office. Briefly I tried to explain to the secretary that I was taking Sheila to the hospital and to have someone find her father and get him there. Time had wound down to that eerie slow-motion pace it assumes in an emergency. Everyone around me seemed to react as if they were in a movie running at an improper speed. What was happening? The junior high aides peered out of the workroom. What was going on? All the time I could feel the warmth of Sheila's blood against my arm, soaking into my shirt as I held her.

Sheila was whiter now. Clad only in her T-shirt and shoes with the towel I had wrapped around her her only other protection, she was getting sluggish, closing her eyes and leaning heavily against me. I ran for my car. Still holding her in my lap, I turned the ignition and jammed the gears into reverse.

"Sheila? Sheila? Stay awake," I whispered, trying to maneuver the car and keep a hold on her at the same time. I should have taken someone with me, I thought absently, but there hadn't been time. No time to tell them what had happened.

"I do be awake," Sheila muttered. Her small fingers dug into my skin, pulling the tender area of my breast painfully tight as she gripped my shirt. "But it hurts."

"Oh, I'm sure it does, baby," I replied. "But keep talking to me, okay?" The distance to the hospital seemed interminable. The traffic impossible. Maybe I should have waited for an ambulance. I had no idea how much blood she had lost, nor how much was too much, nor what I could do about it. I cursed myself for never having followed through on my Red Cross training.

"My Unca Jerry, he said he was going to love me. He said he was going to show me how grown-up people loved each other." Her voice sounded small and childlike. "He

169

said I better know how grown-up people loved. And when
I screamed, he said nobody ain't gonna never love me if I
can't learn how."

"Your Uncle Jerry doesn't know anything, lovey. He
doesn't know what he's talking about."

She caught her lips in a tearless sob. "He said that be
how you and Chad loved each other. He said if I want
you and Chad to love me, I had to let him show me how
so I'd learn."

We neared the hospital. "Oh lovey, he's wrong. Chad
and I love you already. He was just saying that so he
could do something wrong to you. He had no right
to touch you like he did. What he said and what he did
were wrong."

Two young orderlies came running down the emergency
ramp with a stretcher. Apparently Mr. Collins had alerted
the hospital of our coming. As I placed Sheila on the
stretcher for the first time she appeared to register pain
and alarm. Moaning, she began to cry loudly but tear
lessly. She refused to let go of my shirt and strug
gled fiercely as the men tried to pry her fingers loose.

"Don't leave me!" she wailed.

"I'm coming right along with you, Sheila. But lie down.
Come on now, let go of me."

"Don't leave me! Don't let them take me away! I want
you to hold me!" In a contorted mass the four of us and
the stretcher moved toward the door. Sheila retained her
terror-wrought grasp on my shirt, ripping the pocket. I did
not know what brought her to life so fully. Perhaps she
was frightened that I would leave her with these strangers
perhaps she could finally feel the extent of the pain. What
ever it was, she fought so valiantly that in the end it was
easier for me to pick her up and hold her again than to
pry her off and listen to her scream.

The emergency room doctor examined her briefly while
I held her on my lap. Her father was still not there, so I
signed a form stating that I would be responsible for emer
gency treatment until her father could be found.

A nurse came in with a needle and gave her a shot.
Sheila had once again become docile and silent, not even
flinching when the needle came. Within a short time after
the shot, I could feel her fingers relaxing and I laid her on
the examining table. Another nurse started an IV in one of

170

her arms while a young Mexican-American intern was hanging a pint of blood above the table. The doctor gestured for me to come away. With a last look at Sheila, who lay with her eyes closed, pale and tiny on the table, I followed the doctor outside the swinging doors. He asked me what had happened and I told him to the best of my knowledge. At that point we saw Sheila's father stumbling down the corridor with the social worker. He was stone drunk.

The doctor explained that Sheila had lost a tremendous amount of blood and they had to stabilize that first. Apparently, from what he could see in the examination, the knife had punctured the vagina wall into the rectum. It was a very serious injury because of the likelihood of infection and the vast damage done. Once they had stabilized her blood level, the doctor believed there would have to be surgical intervention. Sheila's father weaved uncertainly beside us as the doctor spoke.

There was no more I could do. Undoubtedly my class back at school was in chaos. If Susannah had seen the blood, Anton would have more on his hands than he could handle alone or even with the other aides. And the children would be alarmed that I had left so suddenly. It was best that I get back to my job. I looked down at my clothes. Blood had stained the entire front of my shirt. The first spot on my Levi's had already dried into a dark blot. I stared at it. I was wearing part of somebody's life on me, little red tablespoons of a liquid more precious than gold. I was made uncomfortable by it, startled by how fragile life really is, reminded too fully of my own mortality.

I was back in school by eleven. When I looked up at the clock and saw how little real time had passed, I was shocked. Less than an hour had passed since I had lifted Sheila off my lap during math and seen the blood. The entire drama had taken place in barely fifty minutes. I had even gone home and changed my clothes before returning to class. I could not fathom that. To me it had felt as if a hundred years had been compressed into that fifty minutes. I had aged much more.

That night I did not go back to the hospital. I had called the doctor after school and he told me that they had just taken her into surgery and she was not yet out. Despite the blood administered, her condition had not stabilized but remained critical. He did not expect her out of the recovery room until quite late. She had been semicomatose most of the day and he doubted that she was aware of who had been present. Sheila would go into intensive care after surgery to make sure the hemorrhaging stopped and she would stabilize before she was moved to the children's ward. I asked if I could come up, explaining I was as close to family as the child probably had aside from her father. He suggested I wait until the next day. She would not be conscious enough to know me tonight and I would be in the way in the intensive care unit. They would make her as comfortable as they could, he assured me.

I asked if her father were still there, but the doctor replied no. They had sent him home shortly after I had gone. He was not sober enough to be coherent. The father's brother, Jerry, had been taken into custody.

In a way I was relieved not to have to go back. It had happened too fast and I could not conceive of the severity of the situation. She had talked to me. She walked all the way from the high school to our room and sat through an hour of class. And she had talked to me during the drive to the hospital. She could not be critically injured. I could not believe it.

The blood-stained shirt and jeans lay in a pile where I had hurriedly changed from them before returning to class in the morning. I put the Levi's to soak in the bathtub, but held the shirt, examining the pocket torn when Sheila had struggled with the emergency room attendants. Gently I folded the shirt and put it in the back of my closet. I could not bring myself to throw it away. Neither could I put it in the sink and wash it. I knew there was too much blood in it and if I did, the water would color. At that moment I was unable to wash the blood out, unable to see the water redden and go down the drain like so much filth. I would not be able to stand that.

After supper Chad came over and I related what had taken place. Chad was explosive. He paced the room at first saying nothing and shaking his head in disbelief. The anguish was not so much in the seriousness of the injury but in how it had happened. Chad raged with hatred, threatening to do physical harm to Jerry. He had no compassion for a man who would do such a thing to a little girl and I was frightened by the change in Chad, having never seen him so angry.

Although I was heartsick about the incident, a strange feeling twinged me. Five months earlier, Sheila had been the abuser and someone else had been the victim. Undoubtedly the boy's parents had felt very much the same way as Chad was now feeling toward Jerry. While it did not by any means excuse the gross inhumanity of the crime, it made me aware that the hurt and damage I had found in Sheila was probably in Jerry too. Neither was innocent, but neither was solely evil either. I was sadly plagued by knowing that Jerry was undoubtedly just as much a victim as Sheila. It made things so much more complicated.

The police called later in the evening and asked if I would come down and give them a statement. Together Chad and I went to the police department. In a gray-painted room at a gray-painted table, I told an officer what had happened in my classroom that morning. I repeated what Sheila had said to me and what I had done. It was a grim recounting of an even more grim occurrence.

During recess the next morning I called the hospital again to see how Sheila was coming along. The doctor's voice was more at ease this time. She had tolerated surgery well and had stabilized in intensive care during the night. By morning she was alert and coherent, so they had transferred her down to the children's ward. I could see her any time I wanted. I asked if her father had been in. The doctor said he had not. Please let her know I would be in right after school let out, I asked. The doctor agreed, his voice warm. She was a tough little kid, he said. Yes, I replied, there weren't any that were tougher.

Perhaps the most difficult task had been explaining what had happened to Sheila to the children in my class. We had already talked about abuse, both physical and sexual, in our room. My kids came from a high-risk population for abuse and I felt it was important for them to know what to do if they found themselves in such a situation or saw it happening to someone else. However, sexual abuse was hard to talk about. In a district where sex education had not made great popular strides in the

173

schools, sexual abuse was taboo. I had worked up an informal unit for my children in which we simply discussed the appropriate and inappropriate ways of being "touched." An adult who held you and hugged you was okay. An adult who held your penis and hugged you was not. We discussed what one should do if that happened, because no one had the right to touch a boy or girl in some places. Neither should they ask to be touched there. We had done the unit in October and had gone over it a few times since. It provided a measure of relief for the kids to be able to talk about those things, expressing fears about not knowing what to do when someone touched them and it felt "funny."

But Sheila's case, I did not know how to handle. Sex and violence together are not good topics for primary-age disturbed children. Yet, I had to say something. They saw us leave so unexpectedly and they did see the blood. Then they saw me return without Sheila. I told them briefly that Sheila had been hurt at home and I had had to take her to the hospital because of it. Beyond that I said nothing.

The children made her get-well cards the next afternoon when I said I had called the hospital and Sheila was in the children's unit and feeling better. Poignant, brightly crayoned messages piled up in the correction basket. The event, however, affected the kids more than I had perceived. At closing time William burst into tears.

"What's wrong?" I asked as I sat down on the floor. The children were gathered around the Kobold's Box with me. William too was there but had suddenly dissolved into tears.

"I'm scared about Sheila. I'm scared she's going to die in the hospital. My grampa went to the hospital once and he died there."

Unexpectedly, Tyler also began to sob. "I miss her. I want her back."

"Hey, you guys," I said. "Sheila's doing really well. That's what I told you after lunch. She's getting better. She won't die or anything."

Tears coursed over Sarah's face although she made no noise. Max began to wail in harmony, although I doubt he had any concept of why everybody else was crying. Even Peter was teary-eyed, despite the fact that he and Sheila were sworn enemies most of the time.

"But you won't let us talk about it," Sarah said. "You never even said Sheila's name all day. It's scary."

"Yeah," Guillermo agreed. "I kept thinking about her all the time and you kept acting like she never was here. I miss her."

I looked at them. Everyone but Freddie and Susannah were in tears. I doubted they were all that loyal to Sheila, but what had happened had frightened everyone. Moreover, it had affected me. I had worried and in an attempt to keep things calm I had said nothing. In my classroom we had spent the better part of seven-and-a-half months learning openness and putting ourselves in other people's places. They had learned too well perhaps, because I could not disguise things from them.

So normal closing exercises went undone; the Kobold's Box was unopened, while I talked to them, telling them how I felt and why I had not been as honest as I usually was. We sat down on the floor, all of us together, and had a roundtable.

"Some things are kind of hard to talk about," I said. "What happened to Sheila is one of those things."

"How come?" Peter asked. "Don't you think we're old enough? That's what my mom always says when she don't want to tell me stuff."

I smiled. "Sort of. And sort of because some things are just hard to talk about. I don't even know why. I guess because they scare us. Even us big people. And when big people get scared about things, they don't like to talk about them. That's one of the problems with being big."

The kids were watching me. I looked at them. Each of them, individually. Tyler with her long, ghoulish throat scars. Beautiful black-skinned Peter. Guillermo, whose eyes never really looked anywhere, even when he was paying attention. Rocking, finger-twiddling Max. Sarah. William. Freddie. And my fairy child, Susannah.

"Remember I told you that Sheila got hurt at home. And remember back when we were talking about the ways people can touch you? I was telling you how sometimes people want to put their hands places on a little kid's body that they have no right to touch."

"Yeah, like down where it's private on you, huh?" said William.

I nodded. "Well, someone in Sheila's family touched

175

her where he shouldn't have and when Sheila got unhappy about it, he hurt her."

Foreheads wrinkled. Their eyes were intent. Even Max stopped rocking.

"What did he do to her?" William asked.

"Cut her." As I listened to myself tell these kids, I wondered if I was doing the right thing. Instinctively I felt I was. Our relationship was grounded in the truth, however bad it might be. Moreover, I could not believe knowing could be worse than not knowing, nor worse than the many things these children had seen already. The fact that nothing in their lives was so bad that it could not be talked about had been a cornerstone in this room. Yet, deep inside of me nagged the knowledge that once again I was breaking the rules that I had been taught, overstepping the boundaries of proven educational and psychological practice. And as in all other times I had done that, the worry came that this occasion might be my downfall, that this time I might hurt more than I helped. The war between safety and honesty raged once more.

"Who done it to her?" asked Guillermo. "Was it her father?"

"No. Her uncle."

"Her Uncle Jerry?" Tyler asked.

I nodded.

For a minute there was silence. Then Sarah shrugged. "Well, at least it wasn't her father."

"That don't make it any better, Sarah," Tyler replied.

"Yeah, it does," Sarah answered. "When I was little, before I came to school, my father sometimes he'd come in my room when my mother was at work and . . ." she paused, looked from Tyler to me, then down at the rug. "Well, he done that kind of stuff. It's worse when it's your father, I think."

"Let's not talk about this anymore, okay?" William said. Fear had creased his brow. He wrung his hands.

"No, I wanna," Sarah said. "I want to know how Sheila is."

"No," William said again. Tears returned to his eyes.

"You're scared, William," Guillermo stated. "What are you scared of?"

I reached a hand out. "Why don't you come over here and sit with me."

He rose and came over. I put an arm around him.

"This is a scary thing to talk about, isn't it?"

He nodded. "There's dust under my bed sometimes if my mom doesn't use the vacuum."

"William, that's off the subject," Peter said.

"That dust scares me. Sometimes I think maybe that used to be people. Maybe it's dead people under my bed."

"That's stupid."

"No, sir. It says right in the Bible, Peter, that you came from dust and you turn to dust after you die. It says so. My mom showed it to me. You ask Torey."

"I don't think that's what the Bible means, William," I said.

"And that might have been people under there, that dust. Might have been my grandpa after he went to the hospital. He might be under my bed now. Maybe it's Sheila."

"No, it's not Sheila. Sheila isn't dead, Will. She's in the hospital and she's going to get better," I replied.

"Torey?" Tyler asked.

"Yes?"

"How come Sheila's uncle did that to her? She just told us the other day that he was nice and played with her. How come he cut her?"

I regarded her. I did not have an answer. No matter how long I waited, an answer did not come to me. "I don't know, Ty."

"Did he have problems?" Sarah asked. "Like my father? They put him in the ward at the state hospital 'cause he had problems. That's what my mother told me. He never came back."

"Yes, I guess you could say he had problems. He didn't understand the right way to touch little girls. Or rather, I suspect he understood, but sometimes people do things without thinking first. They just do what sounds good to them at the moment."

"Is he going to go to the state hospital like my father?"

"I don't know. It's against the law to hurt people."

"When's Sheila coming back?" Peter asked.

"As soon as she's better."

"Will she be the same?"

"What do you mean?" I asked.

Peter frowned. "Well, if she got cut down there will she be the same?"

"I'm still not following you, Peter. Explain what you mean."

He hesitated, glanced nervously around the group, back at me. "Can I say some dirty words? I got to so you'll know what I'm talking about. I need to use dirty words."

I nodded. "This is different than yelling them at people. They aren't dirty when they mean something. Go ahead."

Again a hesitation. "Well, down there, that's a girl's cunt, isn't it?"

"Yeah."

"And down there, that's where a girl goes to the bathroom. Well, what if he cut her there? That's where babies come out. What if he cut her there?"

I still did not have the exact question Peter was asking. I decided to turn the question back on him to see if I could pull further information out of him. "What if he did cut her, Peter? What do you think would happen?"

His eyes widened with anxiety. "What if she grows up and has babies?"

"What if she does?"

There were tears in his eyes. "She might crap on them when they're being born." His mouth pulled down in a sob. "That's what my mom done to me. That's why I'm crazy."

"Oh, Peter, that's not true," I said.

He came crawling over on his hands and knees. I was sitting cross-legged on the floor with William against my right side. Peter laid his head in my lap. "Yes, it is."

"No, it isn't. I don't know where you got that idea, but it's wrong."

"Peter, you're not crazy," William said. "Nobody's really crazy. That's just a word. Isn't it, Torey? Just a word. And nobody's a word."

We talked a long time. The bell to go home rang, the buses came and went and we talked. About sexual abuse. About Sheila. About ourselves.

Afterward, I loaded all eight of them into the hatch of my car and drove them home. We never lost the seriousness of the discussion. Even in the car, the questions kept coming. No one ever kidded or made a joke or goofed off. The things we had to talk about were not funny to anyone. The need to talk about them surpassed all other needs that afternoon. And all our differences.

After I had dropped the other children off I collected the get-well notes and a few books I knew Sheila especially liked, and headed for the hospital. She had been placed in an observation room right off the nurses' station and the doorway I was to use was pointed out to me. I entered.

She was alone in the large room with glass windows on one whole wall, like a cage at the zoo. She was lying in a crib with high metal sides. An IV dangled above one post and next to it a unit of blood. The arm that the needles were in was tied to a rung of the crib with a restraint to immobilize it. She looked so young and small.

Tears filled my eyes before I could stop them and they spilled over my cheeks. The only thing I could think of was why had they put her in a crib? Sheila had a lot of dignity for a little kid. I knew that would humiliate her. I knew she would be embarrassed to have me see her in it. Why hadn't they given her a bed like a nearly seven-year-old child should have? Not a crib. Cribs were for babies.

Sheila turned her head toward me when I entered. In silence she regarded me. "Don't cry, Torey," she said softly. "It don't hurt much. Really it don't."

Humble in the presence of such courage, I stared at her. "Why did they put you in a crib?" I asked, my mind blank. I let down the side nearest me and touched her free hand. "You shouldn't be in a crib."

"I don't mind really," she said. I knew that was not true. We had been friends long enough for me to know the extent of her carefully guarded sense of self. She smiled softly, as if I were the one to be comforted, and reached up to touch my face. "Don't cry, Torey. I don't mind."

"It makes me feel better. You scared me so much and I was so worried about you, Sheil. It makes me feel better to cry a little bit and I can't help it."

"It don't really hurt bad." Her eyes had lost some of their expression. Perhaps the medication was causing the glassy effect. "But I do get sort of scared sometimes. Just a little bit. Like last night, I didn't know where I was at. That was kind of scary. But I didn't cry none or anything. And pretty soon the nurse comed over and talked to me. She be right nice to me. But I still be a little scared. I wanted my Pa."

"I bet so. We'll see if we can't get someone to be with you when you get scared."

"I want my Pa."

"I know, honey. And he'll be here when he can."

"No sir. He don't like hospitals none."

"Well, we'll see."

"I want you to stay with me."

I nodded. "I will as much as I can. And Anton will come sometimes too. And I know Chad will want to. He's been asking all day about how you are. We'll do the best we can. I don't want you to get scared, love. I'll try my hardest to help."

She turned her head away from me for a moment and looked up at the IV. "My arm hurts some." Her eyes wandered back to me and suddenly the hurt and the fear were alive in them. Her face contorted in a grimace. "I want you to hold me," she whimpered. "My arm hurts fierce bad and I do be so lonely. I want you to stay here and hold me and not go away."

"Kitten, I don't think they would like me to hold you. I think it'd mess up all the stuff they have hooked up to you. I can hold your hand, if you want."

"No," she whined. "I want you to hold me. I hurt."

I smoothed back her hair and leaned close to her. "Oh I know you do, sweetheart, and I want to. But we can't."

She looked at me a long moment and then that glaze of control filmed over her eyes. She took a deep, shuddery breath and that was all. Once again she was passive, locking up one more thing she could not bear to feel.

"I brought some books. Maybe you'd like me to read to you. It might take your mind off things."

Slowly she nodded. "Read me about the fox and the little prince and his rose."

CHAPTER 17

SHEILA REMAINED IN THE HOSPITAL THROUGH the rest of the month of April. During that time her uncle was arraigned and tried for sexual abuse. He returned to prison. Her father didn't go to see her the entire time she was hospitalized, pleading a phobia of hospitals. Instead he drowned his fears at Joe's Bar and Grill. I went every night after school to see her and usually stayed through dinner. Chad came up most evenings and played checkers with Sheila even after I had left. Anton visited regularly and Whitney was allowed on the unit for a couple brief stops even though she was underage. Oddly, even Mr. Collins came to see Sheila and I surprised him one Saturday afternoon playing a game with her. To the astonishment of the hospital staff Sheila turned out to be one of the most popular children on the unit with a whole entourage of well-wishers coming and going each day. I was thankful for the interest shown in her because much as I wanted to, I could not afford to spend more than a couple of hours up there every night. Yet I knew that I probably would have stayed longer if no one else had shown up.

In a way the hospitalization was good for her. Being so

physically attractive and having come through such a harrowing experience, she was the darling of the nursing staff. They showered her with attention. Sheila responded delightedly. She was cheerful and cooperative in most instances and, of course, never cried. Best of all, she was getting three balanced meals a day and was beginning to put on much-needed weight. It was not until the very end of her hospital stay that she began to get restless, not wanting to stay in bed, and getting cranky with those who insisted she did. Her emotional problems seemed totally eclipsed by this event. Certainly for as severely disturbed a child as she had been, there was almost no evidence of her acting up in the hospital. To the contrary the nurses were forever commenting on her outstanding behavior. This concerned me. While it made the stay more pleasant for everyone, I knew neither the hospitalization itself nor the reason she had gone in were anything other than vastly traumatic events. I feared that like her absurd ability to keep from crying, she had sublimated this misery, making it seem as if it had never happened. That was to me a greater indicator of the seriousness of her disturbance than anything else.

In the meantime the rest of the children had adjusted to life without Sheila. We enjoyed the April sunshine and the resurrecting earth around us. Things calmed down and, except for weekly letters to her, Sheila ceased to be a major topic of conversation.

During this time I learned for certain that my class would be disbanded permanently. A number of things had contributed to that situation and I had been aware of all of them. First, the district was doing some shuffling within itself and now felt that placement of many disturbed children such as Freddie and Susannah could be accomplished without maintaining another separate class as had been done this year. Second, the others had all made enough progress that, realistically, they could go into a less restrictive placement. Perhaps most important, rumblings were coming down of a new bill in Congress on mainstreaming handicapped children back into the normal classrooms. In response to this federal law, a number of special rooms were being eliminated altogether in an attempt to free some specially trained teachers for consultation to the regular classroom. As I had the most severe level, those in charge of placement were most interested in eliminating my level entirely. And last, and certainly most consequential, money was running tight. Maintaining children in classes like mine was very expensive. The low ratio of children to teachers, the greater training of the teachers who could thus command higher salaries, the special equipment all cost a great deal of money. The district could not afford to run as many special classes in the future as they had this year.

While I was saddened by the news, it was not unexpected. My sadness was only the same one I felt every year as it drew to a close and I wished we could start all over. In fact I had my own personal plans. The school district had offered me another position; however, I had applied to graduate school and had been accepted. I already possessed a master's degree in special education and my regular teaching certificate. But I did not have full certification for teaching special children. While the state was not yet requiring this full certificate in addition to the regular certification, I could see it on the horizon. Too many good teachers I had known had lost their jobs simply because they had not been able to keep up with the certification requirements. If the day came and I found myself in a job that I did not want to give up to go back to school, I would not want to be caught short of credits. This job was essentially over; I wouldn't be able to go back to the same kids and the same class in the fall anyway; so now seemed as good a time as any to return to school.

I was also toying with the idea of pursuing a doctorate. I had become increasingly involved in research during the previous years and had been appalled by the huge gaps in research in the areas of childhood withdrawal and depression.

While I loved teaching, the months just past had been filled with soul-searching about my future. In addition, Chad was renewing pressure to marry and settle down. That night after the trial with Sheila had affected him and he now openly acknowledged he wanted a family. Yet I was getting restless. When the acceptance from the university had come on April sixth, I had agreed to go,

183

which meant when school let out in June, I would be moving half a continent away from Chad and Sheila and a place that had given me several of the best years of my life.

Sheila returned to school early in May. She came back with the same extroverted gusto she had displayed in the hospital, giving the distinct impression that she had been on an extended holiday. As I watched her resume her old place in the class I was more unsettled than ever by her attitude. One could not swallow that much pain and get away with it. I feared she might be even more disturbed than I had thought; that perhaps she was slipping off into some fantasy to protect herself from the horrors of the real world. But throughout the day and then the next couple of days she gave no indication of any problem. For all the world she seemed like some normal child who had stopped by to participate in our classroom activities.

By the end of the week the veneer was beginning to wear thin. The old hassles had begun to raise their heads again. I started demanding more out of her and she found herself making mistakes. This put her in a sulk for a few hours on Thursday. The other kids were readjusting to her return and were not giving her the attention to which she had grown so accustomed. This provoked a bit of angry fussing when things did not go her way. But most important she slowly began to talk to me again. That, I decided, was what had been missing. While she kept up a constant chatter in school and after, she never really did say anything. It was all just prattle over the immediate situation. Unlike before when she was open and voluntarily brought up her feelings, now she spoke only about safe things. Bit by bit, however, a statement would creep in that mirrored what was below the carefree surface.

She had returned to school wearing the old overalls and T-shirt. The blood stains were still visible and after having gained weight in the hospital, Sheila was too large to wear the overalls comfortably. They were too short and too tight. I wondered what had become of the red-and-white dress, so finally on Friday evening after school, I asked. Sheila was helping me cut out figures for the bulletin board; so we sat together at one table, the work spread between us.

She pondered my question a moment. "I ain't gonna wear it no more."

"How come?"

"That day . . ." she paused, concentrating on her cutting. "The day my Unca Jerry . . . Well, he says it be a right pretty dress. He could feel under it. He done it before but this time he wouldn't stop. He kept putting his hands under there. So I ain't wearing it no more. I ain't having nobody feel there."

"Oh."

"Besides, it got all blooded up. My Pa, he throwed it away when I was gone."

A long, heavy silence fell between us. I did not know what to say next so I just continued to work on what I was cutting out. Sheila looked up. "Torey?"

"Hmm?"

"Do you and Chad ever do that stuff together? Like Unca Jerry did to me?"

"What your uncle did to you, no one should do. That was wrong. Having intercourse is something grown-up people do with each other. It's not something kids do. And no one ever uses a knife. That was wrong."

"I know what it is. My Pa, he brings home ladies sometimes and does that. He thinks I be asleep but I ain't. It makes a lot of noise, so I wake up. I seen them. I know what it is."

Her eyes were cloudy. "Is it really love?"

I took a long breath. "You're not really old enough, Sheil, to understand altogether. Sometimes it's called love. But it isn't exactly. It's sex. Uually two people do it when they really love one another and then it's good and they like it. But sometimes people just do it but they don't love each other. It's still sex, but it's not love. Sometimes a person forces another to do it. And that's always wrong."

"I ain't never gonna love anybody if I have to do that."

"You're too little. Your body isn't ready to do those sorts of things yet, so it hurts you. But it isn't love, Sheil. Love is different. Love is a feeling. What happened was a really wrong thing. No one should do that to a little girl. It hurt you because it was not something that should have happened. You're too little."

"Then why did he do it to me, Torey?"

Putting down the figure I had been cutting, I pushed

back my hair. "You're asking me awfully hard questions, sweetheart."

"But I can't understand that. I liked Unca Jerry. He played with me. Why did he want to hurt me?"

"I don't really know. Sometimes people just lose control. Like remember you and me back in February when I went to the conference? I mean we sort of did that to each other. It's something that happens."

Sheila stopped her cutting, letting the paper and scissors drop through her fingers to the tabletop. For a long, silent moment she sat motionless, staring at the paper and scissors and at her still spread hands. Her chin quivered. "Things never are the way you really want them to be, are they?" She did not look at me.

I did not respond, not knowing how to.

She lay her face down on the table in a gesture of defeat. "I don't wanna be me anymore. I just don't."

"Sometimes it's hard," I replied, still not knowing what to say but feeling the need to say something.

She turned her head so she could see me but let it remain on the table midst the shambles of her cutting. Her eyes were dull. "I wanna be somebody like Susannah Joy and have lots of nice dresses to wear. I don't wanna be here. I wanna be a regular kid and go to a regular kid's school. I just do not want to be me anymore. I'm sick of it. But I can't figure out how to do it."

I watched her. Somehow I always think I have finally lost my innocence. I always think, my God, I've seen the worst, the next time it isn't going to hurt me as bad. And I always find it does.

CHAPTER 18

I DECIDED AS A LAST MAJOR ACTIVITY OF THE school year, our class would put on a Mother's Day program. One of the greatest tragedies to befall special education is that the special children almost never get to participate in the traditional fun activities of regular children. For the special kids, just getting through from day to day seems to be enough of an achievement. But I always hated that. Just "getting through from day to day" makes for a life hardly worth living. We all know it's the icing and not the cake that causes most people to eat cake. So I tried to make up for it by creating some of the more popular activities of the regular school program in our room.

We had had an assembly for the families in October that had gone off . . . not too badly. So I decided that was just what we needed to perk up May. To devise a program that children like Susannah and Freddie and Max could participate in was no easy task. But with the help of my parents' group we put together a few songs, a poem or two, and a skit full of the traditional spring flowers and mushrooms that always seem to bloom in small children's plays.

The kids were all excited about the event, except that Peter wanted to do a more ambitious skit. Most of them had just seen *The Wizard of Oz* on its umpteenth yearly run on television and were determined we should do that. I explained that with only five reliable actors that might be a bit difficult especially since no one except Sheila could read much. Peter in particular was adamant that he would not be any woodland flower and instead he wanted to be a Tin Man. Sarah agreed. Out on the playground they had been playing *Wizard of Oz* and she thought it went very nicely. I finally gave in, stating that if Peter and Sarah could develop a rough skit that would include parts for Freddie and the others, and Guillermo could play a good part despite his handicap, I would let them do it.

So we began practicing. Actually we had started working on the songs back in April, but Peter's change in script did not occur until Sheila was back with us in May. Obviously, our Mother's Day play was going to be a little late. I was eternally grateful for Sheila and her agile memory. She had a reasonable singing voice and could remember anything she was given. So I padded the program with her and with Max, whose disturbance had equipped him with the ability to repeat vast quantities of materials, although not necessarily on demand.

I had asked Sheila if she wanted her father to attend. Many of the other fathers were coming, since although the play was billed as a Mother's Day show, it was one of the only opportunities parents had of seeing their kids in a joyful and frivolous school activity. Besides, I wanted all the families to feel free to attend any of our school functions. So I asked Sheila about her father, knowing that if she wanted him, special arrangements would have to be made to get him there.

She screwed up her face a moment in consideration. "He wouldn't come."

"Anton could go out and get him, if he wanted to come. As long as we know ahead of time, it wouldn't be hard."

"I don't think he'd come anyways. He don't like school stuff too good."

"But he could see you in the play and singing your song. I bet your Dad would be proud to see you do all those things." I sat down on one of the little chairs so that

188

I would be more at her level. "You know, Sheil, you've really come a long ways in here since January. You're like a different girl. You don't get into trouble nearly as much as then."

She nodded her head emphatically. "I used to wreck stuff all the time. But I don't anymore. And I used to not talk when I got mad. I used to be a bad girl."

"You've done a lot better, alright. And you know what? I bet your Pa would like to see how well you've done. I think he'd be proud of you because I don't think he realizes what an important girl you are in this class."

Sheila ruminated a moment while studying me through squinted eyes. "Maybe he would come."

I nodded. "Maybe he would."

The morning of the program Chad arrived in the classroom carrying a big box. Anton was setting up props and Sheila was brushing her teeth. "What are you doing here?" I asked, surprised to see him.

"I came to see Sheila."

Excitedly, Sheila leaped down from the chair she was standing on and ran over.

"Spit out your toothpaste first," Chad warned her. She scurried back to the sink to return in seconds, toothpaste still outlining her lips. "I understand you're going to have a play today."

"Yeah!" she cried, bouncing around him in excitement. "I'm gonna be Dorothy and Torey's gonna braid my hair up in pigtails. An' I'm gonna sing a song and say a poem, and my Pa's gonna be here and *watch* me!" She was out of breath after the exclamation, having said it so rapidly. "Are you gonna come?"

"Nope. But I brought you a good-luck present for your debut."

Sheila's eyes widened. "Me?"

"Yes, you."

In glee she hugged his knees with such gusto that Chad wobbled unsteadily.

I knew what was inside the box—a long dress, red, white and blue with lace around the front placket. A beautiful and expensive dress that Chad had brought back with him from a recent trip to New York. I had told Chad about what had happened to the other dress and

189

about Sheila's feeling that dresses made her too vulnerable. For that reason he had bought a long dress instead of a short one. The night he had come in to show me the dress, his eyes were all sparkly like a little boy's. I could just picture him in the New York stores, his tall football player's frame towering over miniature racks of little girls' dresses; his arms spread wide attempting to describe for the salesclerk the special little girl back in Iowa for whom he needed that very special dress. Chad had great confidence that he had found just what Sheila would dream for. That it would erase the horror of the last month and recapture at least a little of the magic we had found the night of the court hearing.

Sheila ripped open the paper and lifted the lid on the box. Momentarily she hesitated, gazing at the tissue paper still partly obscuring the contents. Very, very slowly she lifted the dress out of the box, her eyes huge and round. She looked at Chad who knelt on the floor next to her.

Then she let it drop back into the box and lowered her head. "I ain't wearing dresses no more," she whispered hoarsely.

Chad turned to me in bewilderment, his own disappointment clear in his face. I came over and knelt down with them. "Don't you think it might be okay this once?"

She shook her head.

I looked at Chad. "I think we need a minute alone, if you'll excuse us." I rose and took Sheila to the far side of the room behind the animal cages. I knew the confusion that must be filling Chad's head. I knew as well that Sheila must have been in torment. She loved pretty things so much and that was a stunning dress Chad had brought, far lovelier than the red-and-white one he had gotten her in March. Yet, what had happened to her was too fresh, the hurt too raw.

Her face contorted into a teary-eyed grimace by the time I had her behind the cages. She pressed her fingers to her temples in an effort to keep the tears back, but for the first time since she had come to my class she was unable to. Over her cheeks coursed rivulets and she dissolved into sobs.

The time had finally come. The time I had been waiting for through all these long months that I knew sooner or later had to occur. Now it was here.

190

For several minutes I sat with her behind the cages. She had surprised me so much by actually crying that for a moment I did nothing but look at her. Then I gathered her into my arms, hugging her tightly. She clutched onto my shirt so that I could feel the dull pain of her fingers digging into my skin. When it became apparent that she had lost all control and was not going to regain it, I picked her up and came out of hiding. I needed to go somewhere where the other kids coming in and all the preparations for the program would not interrupt us.

"What did I do?" Chad asked worriedly, his gentle face distorted with concern. "I didn't mean . . ."

I shook my head. "Don't worry about it. Put the dress over there. I'll get back to you after a bit, okay?" I turned to Anton. "Can you take care of things for a while?"

The only place I could think of where we would be entirely alone and undisturbed was the book closet. Attempting to manipulate a kiddie chair along with me while carrying Sheila, I unlocked the closet and went in, securing the door behind me. I put the chair against a stack of reading books and sat down, shifting Sheila to make her more comfortable.

She sobbed hard, but not in the hysterical manner in which she had started. But she cried and cried and cried. I simply held her and rocked the chair back and forth on its rear legs, feeling my arms and chest get damp from the tears and her hot breath and the smallness of the room. At first my mind was busy, wondering how Anton was managing alone with all the kids so high about the play, thinking about the program itself and how it would go, mulling over Sheila's situation. After a while my mind ran dry and I just sat and rocked, thinking of nothing in particular, except that my arms were getting tired.

Ultimately the tears stopped. Sheila had been reduced to a quivery, soggy lump. All her muscles had relaxed from exhaustion. The little room was humid and overly warm and both of us were awash with the saliva and tears and mucus that crying always brings. I smoothed her damp hair back from her face and wondered what had happened in her head to make Chad's gift the final snapping point.

"Do you feel a little better?" I asked gently.

She did not reply but lay against me. Her body convulsed with the hiccupy gasps and shudders that are the aftermath of hard crying. "I'm gonna throw up."

My teacher's reflexes came instantly into action and I let us out of the book closet and into the girls' restroom around the corner. When she came out of the toilet stall she looked battle-weary, her face red and swollen, her steps tottery. Faint lines of toothpaste were still visible on her chin. I picked her up.

"Sometimes that happens," I said as we returned to our haven in the closet. "Sometimes when you cry real hard, it makes you sick."

She nodded. "I know."

We had only the one chair between us but she willingly clung to my lap, leaning heavily against my soggy shirt. We sat for a while saying nothing.

"I can hear your heart beat," she said at last.

I touched her head gently. "Do you think we ought to go back to class? It must be the middle of math period by now."

"No."

Again silence drifted around us. A million things were running through my head, none of them finding words.

"Tor?"

"Yes?"

"Why did he buy me that dress?"

Across my mind trickled the thought that perhaps Sheila believed Chad had gotten her the dress for the same reason that her Uncle Jerry had told her he liked her red-and-white one. What a horrible thought that must have been for her; safe, kind, lovable Chad wanting her in a dress so he could have the same access to her that Uncle Jerry had had. It was no more than speculation on my part, but it made me certain not to reply that Chad had done it for "love."

"Because I told him your other one was ruined. He thought you might like something pretty to wear in the play." I ran my fingers through her silky hair. "I forgot to tell him you weren't wearing dresses anymore. That was my fault."

She did not respond.

"You know, don't you, that Chad would never do things to you like your Uncle Jerry did. He knows you shouldn't do those things to little girls. He didn't bring the dress to hurt you. He wouldn't ever hurt you."

"I know it. I didn't mean to cry."

"Oh, sweetie, that's okay. Chad knows that things have been hard for you. No one minds that you cry. Sometimes that's the only way to make things better. We all know that. Nobody cares if you cry."

"I wanted the dress," she said softly, pausing. "I wanted it. I just got scared, that's all. And I couldn't stop."

"That's okay. It really is. Chad knows what little girls are like. We all do."

"I don't know why I cried. I don't know what happened."

"Don't worry about it."

The pressure of being gone so long when I knew the children would be excited about the play was getting the better of me. "Sheil, I have to go back to the room. The kids are all there and Anton's by himself. I have two ideas for you. You can come back with me or maybe if you don't feel up to it you could go down to the nurse's office and rest awhile."

"Do I gotta go home 'cause I throwed up?"

"No. You're not sick or anything."

She slid off my lap. "Can I rest a little? I'm tired."

I explained to the secretary that Sheila needed to lie down but didn't need to be sent home and I would be back in half an hour at recess to check on her. The secretary gave us a blanket and I settled Sheila down on one of the cots.

"Torey?" she asked as I tucked the blanket around her. "Do you suppose I could still have the dress? I wouldn't really mind wearing it."

I nodded and smiled. "Yeah. Chad left it for you."

I came back to the office at recess time and Sheila was asleep. She slept the rest of the morning until I came down and woke her for lunch.

With good reason both L. Frank Baum and Judy Garland probably turned in their graves that May afternoon. Except for bearing the same title and characters as the famed story, the children's production had little in common with the book or the movie.

Sheila played Dorothy mostly by virtue of her ability to think fast and make up dialogue quickly. Both Tyler and Sarah had wanted the part, which resulted in some not-too-good-natured arguing for a while and a near-split of the Sarah-Peter production team. But Peter seemed to have authority in casting parts and he selected Sheila. Tyler was given the ignominious task of portraying all of the wicked witches. Sarah was transformed into the Scarecrow. William played the Cowardly Lion and Guillermo was the Wizard himself. Oddly, Peter selected Susannah to play the Good Witch Glenda, another fought-over part. The only reason for his choice I could think of was that Susie was so delicately pretty that she made a very realistic fairy even without a costume; but Peter had his own reasons that he would not disclose. Freddie was the sole Munchkin and Max a lone winged monkey. Peter, of course, was the Tin Man.

Only parents, teachers or folks with an uncanny love of unintentionally funny children would have properly appreciated *The Wizard of Oz* as produced by my class. Sheila had fully recovered from her troubles in the morning and had donned the dress Chad brought, refusing to wear the costume Whitney had made for her. Refreshed by a two-hour nap, she bounced all over as she spoke, knocking over scenery and props. Freddie on the other hand would not move. He simply sat in his place, a ridiculous Munchkin hat stuck on his head, and waved at his mother in the audience. His fat legs tripped Sheila on one occasion causing her to fall into his lap. At last Anton had to drag him off when his part was over. The Cowardly Lion was typecasting for William and perhaps because he knew the feeling of fear so well, he gave the truest performance of all, quivering and quaking about on the stage. Most surprising, Susannah Joy did quite well as Glenda. She drifted onto the stage and floated around as out of touch with reality as always, muttering to herself in a high-pitched little squeak. But in the setting of the play, it looked astonishingly natural.

The only major problem suffered during the course of the play was when Sheila got long-winded in her dialogue and often felt the need to narrate parts of the play in case the audience hadn't figured out for themselves what was happening. This left everyone else standing around dumbly while Sheila launched into lengthy monologues. Finally Peter walked out onto the stage during one of her soliloquies and told her to get off.

The remainder of the program was delightful. No one forgot their lines in the poems and the songs were sung with rousing, albeit off-key, gusto. Afterwards we had cookies and punch while the children showed their parents things they had done in school.

Sheila's father did come. Dressed in the tattered suit that buckled over his tremendous stomach and reeking, once again, of cheap after-shave, he had eased his mammoth bulk into one of the tiny chairs. All through the program I kept praying it would not break as it creaked ominously with his weight shifts. For the first time I saw him smile at his daughter when she came bounding over to him after the first performance. He had had the kindness to come sober and appeared to enjoy being with us. He never commented about Sheila's new dress until I finally came over and told him toward the end of the party that Chad had bought it for her. He regarded his daughter carefully and then turned to me, pulling out a worn wallet from his coat pocket.

"I ain't got much here," he said quietly. I was terror-stricken, thinking that he was going to offer to pay for the dress and knowing it was obviously an expensive item. But he had other ideas. "If I give you money, would you take Sheila to buy some everyday clothes? I know she needs something and, well, you need a woman for that kind of thing . . ." his voice trailed off and he averted his eyes. "If I keep hold of the money . . . well, I got a little problem, you know. I was wondering . . ." He had ten dollars in his hand.

I nodded. "Yes, I will. I'll take her out after school next week."

He smiled at me, his lips pressed tight together in a faint, sad smile. Then before I knew it, he was gone. I stared at the bill. Not much clothing could be bought for that anymore. But he had tried. In his own way he had tried to make sure that the money went where it was supposed to before it went for a bottle. I liked the man

behavior continued to deteriorate as a result of increasing neurological destruction. He was too violent and disruptive, his behaviors too impulsive for anything but a tightly structured classroom. Guillermo's family was planning to move. And Max, Freddie and Susannah would all go to special programs. Freddie was being placed in a room for the severely and profoundly retarded, and the teacher hoped he would not be too much of a problem. She had been over to observe him several times to see how his behavior was managed in our class. Max was doing beautifully. He was using much more normal speech and less echolalia. Both he and Susannah were going to a special program for autistic children.

And Sheila? Sheila. I had not spoken with her yet about the impending termination of class. I had put it off because I did not know what would happen when I did tell her. In short, I was scared. She had come a long way from that frightened little lump that was dragged into our room in January; far from the dependent belt-hanger of February. Jimmie had been forgotten and she almost never referred to being put on the highway anymore. But she was fragile. I did not think she would need a special classroom any longer. In fact, I feared she'd be ignored in one because she was so verbal and able to look out for herself. I was afraid that to place her in one now would force her to readopt some negative behavior just to get the share of attention she required. What she needed was simply someone who cared. I was tentatively thinking of suggesting to Ed that she be advanced to third grade, even though she was small, so she would be closer academically and socially to the other children. Despite her emotional problems, she was mature for her age. Besides, I had a good friend teaching third grade on the other side of town. The district would bus her there if requested because it was closer to the migrant camp than my school was and because maintaining her in a regular classroom was much less expensive than in a special one. And Sandy would take good care of Sheila for me. That assurance I needed for myself.

In an attempt to see Sheila into regular classroom life, I decided to mainstream her into a second grade class in our school for math. One of the second grade teachers, Nancy Ginsberg, was a pleasant, dedicated woman who had been among the first to invite my class and me to share activities with her group. So I approached her one afternoon in the lounge and asked if she would be willing to take Sheila for math. I explained that Sheila was considerably advanced beyond second grade math, but I wanted her out of the room for a period or so during the day in order that she could become readjusted to the strain of a regular classroom. Math was her most secure subject, so that seemed the best place to start. Nancy agreed.

"Guess what?" I said to Sheila as we were putting away toys from freetime.

"What?"

"You're going to do something neat from now on. You're going to go into a regular class for part of the day."

She looked up sharply. "Huh?"

"I talked to Mrs. Ginsberg and she said you could come have math in her room each day."

"Like William does?"

"That's right."

She bent back over the pieces of an Erector set she was putting away. "I don't wanna."

"You're just not used to the idea. You'll want to. Just think, it'll be a regular class. Remember once, you told me that you wished you were in a regular class? Now you will be."

"I ain't going."

"Why not?"

"This here be my class. I ain't going in nobody else's class."

"It's just for math."

Her nose wrinkled. "But that's my favorite in here. It ain't fair you make me leave my favorite time in here."

"You can have math in here too, if you want. But you'll have math in Mrs. Ginsberg's room too, starting on Monday."

"No, I ain't."

Sheila was not keen on the idea at all. For every reason I had, she had a counter reason. The rest of the day she alternately sulked and stormed, not letting me ever change the subject. By afternoon I had had enough and flatly stated that I had heard all the protests out of her I wanted to hear. She was going, she had two days to get ready and I would do all I could to make the change easier, but she was going.

Sheila stomped her feet angrily and stalked off to rattle the bars on Onions' cage. After listening to the persistent clatter of the cage, which Onions fortunately was not in at the time, I went over and dragged her to the table, giving her the alternative of getting her act together better or sitting in the quiet corner. At that Sheila sprung to her feet and marched defiantly off to the quiet corner. Banging the chair around, she sat.

I let her sit. I went back to helping William with his art project and ignored her. She sat the remainder of the afternoon despite both Anton and my telling her she could leave if she calmed down, and even Sarah's offering to let her help with afternoon snacks.

Since she was obviously interested in making me feel bad, I left her with Anton after school and went down to the teachers' lounge to make lesson plans. If Sheila got into one of her moods, she was best left alone. When I returned just before five, she was lounging on a pillow reading a book.

"You done being mad?" I asked.

She nodded casually, not looking up from the book. "You're going to be sorry you made me go."

"And what is that supposed to mean?"

"I ain't going to be good if I have to go. I'm gonna be bad and she'll send me back here. Then you can't make me leave anymore."

"Sheila," I said in exasperation, "think about that one a while. That's not what you want to do."

"Yes, it is," she replied, still not looking up from her reading.

I glanced at the clock. It was dangerously close to the time when she had to leave. I hated it when she was like this. Coming over to where she was sitting, I dropped on my knees beside her. "What's up, kiddo? Why don't you want to go? I thought you'd like it, being in a regular class again."

She shrugged.

I lifted the book out of her hands so that she had to

look at me. "Sheil, I want your thoughts. You know I can't send you in there if you're going to cause trouble. You got me on that one because I don't want Mrs. Ginsberg to have problems. But you can't want to do this."

"I do."

"Sheil . . ."

She finally looked directly at me, her blue eyes fluid. "How come you don't want me in here no more?"

"I never said that. I want you in here. Of course I want you in here. But I want you to learn what's happening in a real class too so you can go back to one."

"I already know what a real class is like. That's where I was before I came here. I wanna be in this crazy class."

The clock edged toward five. "Sheil, listen, we're out of time. You're going to have to run to catch the bus as it is. I'll talk to you more about it tomorrow."

Sheila would not discuss it further and she was true to her word. I sent her off on Monday morning for thirty-five minutes in Mrs. Ginsberg's class. Within fifteen minutes Anton had to go retrieve her. She had ripped up papers, thrown pencils and tripped some poor unsuspecting second grader twice her size. Anton came dragging her in kicking and screaming. The second the door shut behind them and they were safely in the classroom, Sheila stopped. A pleased smile touched her lips. I sank into a chair beside Max and covered my eyes while Anton escorted her to the quiet corner.

Because her behavior made me extremely angry and I did not trust myself for a while, and also because I knew the time had come to discuss the whole matter of what was going to happen to her the next year, I did not confront her immediately about her behavior in Mrs. Ginsberg's room. After I had calmed down I told her she could leave the corner and rejoin us and then I went about our normal routine.

Directly defying me apparently frightened Sheila considerably. The remainder of the day she was oversolicitous toward me, trying to make sure I saw how good she was being. Also, the fact that I did not deal with the infraction except for the quiet-corner stay was novel, and this troubled Sheila even more. She asked me once when

201

I was going to get mad at her. I smiled, not wanting her to think that my sudden indifference was another indicator of my desire to be rid of her. So I told her we'd discuss the matter later when we had more time. But she was nervous the rest of the day, shadowing me from a distance.

I walked out to the buses with the other children after school. When I returned to the room Sheila stood against the far wall by the animal cages, her eyes wide and fearful. I jerked my head in the direction of one of the tables. "Come over here, kiddo. I think it's time we talked."

Hesitantly she approached, sitting in a chair across the table from me. Her face expressed her wariness, her eyes dilated. "You mad at me?"

"About this morning? I sure was this morning, but I'm not now. No, I just want to find out what is going on with you. I don't really understand why you don't want to go. Last week you refused to talk to me about it. So I just want to find out. You usually have good reasons for what you do; I trust you in that way."

She studied me.

"Well?"

"This here be my class," she replied, falling back on the word "be" which had become almost extinct.

"Yes, it is. I'm not trying to kick you out of it. That's just thirty-five minutes out of a whole day. Besides, I think it's time that you start thinking about a regular class for next year."

"I ain't going in no regular class. This here be my class."

I regarded her a long moment. "Sheil, it's May. The school year will be over in a few weeks. I think it's time to think about next year."

"I'm going to be in here next year."

My heart was sinking. "No," I replied softly.

Her eyes flashed. "I am too! I'll be the baddest kid in the whole world. I'll do terrible things and then they'll make you keep me. They won't let you make me go away."

"Oh, Sheil," I wailed.

"I ain't going anywheres else. I'll be bad again."

"It isn't like that, kitten. I'm not kicking you out. God,

202

Sheila, listen to me, would you?" She had her hands over her ears.

She raised her stormy eyes to me. They were angry and hurt-looking, the old flare of revenge glinting in them.

"This class isn't going to be here next year," I said so softly that it came out almost inaudibly. Yet she heard it through her hands.

Like a wave the expression on her face changed and she lowered her hands. The anger drained away leaving her pale. "What d'you mean? Where's it going?"

"This class won't be here. The school district decided they didn't need it. Everybody can go to other classes."

"Didn't need it?" she shouted. "Of course they need it! I need it! I'm still crazy. I need a crazy kidses class. So does Peter. And Max. And Susie. We're all still crazy kids."

"No, Sheil, you're not. I'm not sure you ever were. But you're not now. It's time to stop thinking that."

"Then I will be. I'll do lots of bad stuff again. I ain't going nowhere."

"Sheil, I'm not going to be here either."

Her face froze.

"I'm moving in June. After school is over, I'm going away. It's really hard for me to say that to you, because I know we've gotten to be such good friends. But the time has come. I don't love you any less and I'm not leaving because of anything you did or didn't do. It's a separate decision I made. A grown-up decision."

She continued to look at me. With elbows on the table, her hands were clasped together and she rested her cheek against her fist. Her underwater-colored eyes studied my face without seeing.

"All things end, Sheil. I'm a teacher, so my ending comes in June. We've had terrific times together and I wouldn't have changed it for anything in the world. You've changed so much. And so have I, really. We've grown together and now it's time to see how good the growing was. I think we're ready. You too. I think you're ready to try it on your own. You're strong enough."

Tears suddenly filled her eyes and spilled over, making fast paths over her round cheeks and down to her chin. Yet she remained motionless and unblinking, her face still propped in her hands. I was running out of words to say. I often forgot she was only six. She would not even be seven until July. I forgot because her eyes were so old.

Slowly she lay her hands on the table and lowered her head. She sat a moment, still not wiping away the tears that continued to fall noiselessly. Then she rose and turned away from me, went over to the far side of the room and sat down amidst the pillows on the floor. Once there she covered her face with her hands. Still no sound came from her.

I sat in silence feeling acutely the pain she radiated, which I suppose was my own pain too. Had I gotten too involved, I wondered? Despite her apparent progress, had I let her grow too dependent on me? Would it have been better to have left her as I found her in January and simply taught her, rather than have accustomed her to the everyday trials of loving someone? I had always been a maverick among my colleagues. I belonged to the better-to-have-loved-and-lost school, which was not a popular notion in education. The courses, the professionals, all preached against getting involved. Well, I could not do that. I could not teach effectively without getting involved, and in my heart, because I did belong to the love-and-lost school, when the end came I could leave. It always hurt, and the more I loved a child, the more it hurt. But when the time came that we had to part or I had to honestly give up on the child because I could do no more, I could go. I could do it because I took with me, every time, the priceless memories of what we had had, believing that there is no more one can give another than good memories. Nothing I could do, even if I worked with Sheila the rest of her school career, could ensure happiness for her. Only she could do that. All I could give her would be my love and my time. When the end came, the parting would be just as painful. In the end my efforts would be reduced once more to memories.

Yet in watching her, I worried that there had not been sufficient time to heal her hurts enough, that she might not be strong enough to tolerate my painful way of teaching. While it was right for me, perhaps I was unfair to her in giving her no choice about it. But what should

204

I have done? My heart ripped with worry that at last I had been given the wrong child, the one I hurt instead of helped. Being a maverick is admissible when one is an academician. When one is a practitioner, it is usually safer to be a conformist.

Slowly I rose and came over to where she sat still noiseless, except for snuffling. "Go away," she stated quietly but firmly through her hands.

"Why? Because you're crying?"

The hands came down and she looked at me briefly. "No." She paused. "Because I don't know what to do."

I sat across from her, arranging a pillow and leaning back on it. For the first time I did not feel like putting my arms around her to soothe away the hurt. Dignity sat as tangible as a cloak about her. We were equals then, not one the older, one the younger. I no longer was the wiser one, the smarter one, the stronger one. We were equal in our humanity.

"How come you ain't staying to make me good?" she asked at last.

"Because it isn't me that makes you good. It's you. I'm only here to let you know that someone cares if you are good or not. That someone cares what happens to you. And it won't matter where I am, I still will always care."

"You're just like my Mama," she said. Her voice was soft and unaccusing, as if she had already resolved how things were and why.

"No, I'm not, Sheil." I regarded her. "Or maybe I am. Maybe leaving you was just as hard for your Mama as it will be for me. Maybe it hurt her that much too."

"She never loved me really. She loved my brother better. She left me on the highway like some dog. Like I didn't even belong to her."

"I don't know about that. I don't know anything about your Mother or why she did what she did to you. And really, Sheila, you don't either. All you know is how it felt to you. But your Mama and I are different. I'm not your Mother. No matter how much you want it to be that way, I'm not."

The tears renewed in intensity. She played with the waistband of her pants. "I know that."

"I knew you did. But I know you dreamed. In the

205

same way, I guess I did too at times. But it never was any more than a dream. I'm your teacher and when the school year ends, I'll just be your friend. But I will be your friend. For as long as you want me, I'll always be that."

She looked up. "What I can't figure out is why the good things always end."

"Everything ends."

"Not some things. Not the bad things. They never go away."

"Yes, they do. If you let them, they go away. Not as fast as we'd like sometimes, but they end too. What doesn't end is the way we feel about each other. Even when you're all grown up and somewhere else, you can remember what a good time we had together. Even when you're in the middle of bad things and they never seem to be changing, you can remember me. And I'll remember you."

Unexpectedly she smiled, just a little smile, and rather sadly. "That's 'cause we tamed each other. Remember that book? Remember how the little boy was mad because he'd gone to all that trouble to tame the fox and now the fox was crying 'cause he had to leave?" She smiled in memory, looking within herself, almost unaware of me. The tears had dried upon her cheeks. "And that fox said it had been good anyways because he would always remember the wheat fields. Remember that?"

I nodded.

"We tamed each other, didn't we?"

"We sure did."

"It makes you cry to tame someone, doesn't it? They kept crying in that book and I never 'xactly knew why. I always thought you only cried when someone hit you."

Again I nodded. "You take a chance at crying when you let someone tame you. That seems to be part of being tamed, I guess."

Sheila pressed her lips together and wiped the last traces of tears from her face. "It still hurts a lot though, don't it?"

"Yeah, it sure still does hurt."

CHAPTER 20

SHEILA WENT BACK TO MRS. GINSBERG'S ROOM the next morning and made it through the thirty-five minutes without too much trouble. Our problems were by no means resolved. Despite Sheila's recognition that the school year was ending and that we would no longer be together, she could not accept it gracefully. I doubted that she would in the two weeks left to us. Her behavior became a little less polished as she vacillated between anger at me for leaving and fear that I was going to. She could not separate out clearly that what was happening to us was different from what had happened between her and her mother. Time and time again we had to discuss the issue in far more detail than her previous conversational obsessions had required. She clung to *The Little Prince* as literary proof that people did part and it did hurt and they did cry, but they all still loved each other. The book was never far from her hands at any time and she could quote parts of it from memory. Because it was in print, it seemed to have more validity to her than my words.

She certainly had learned to cry. Most of the next days found her in tears or on the verge of them. Her eyes were almost like leaky faucets after a while; tears streamed over her cheeks even when she was smiling or playing. When questioned about them she often did not know why she was crying. I let the tears run and did not worry about them. So long had passed since she had cried that I believed she had to accustom herself to it, finding the width and breadth of the emotion, and if it helped her to prepare for what lay ahead, so much the better. Slowly the tears began to disappear.

Underneath it all her marvelous core of joy and courage gleamed. This was her hardest task. All else that had happened in her life had not been voluntary and she had had no choice but to let it happen and try to survive in the aftermath. But she knew this was coming and she struggled valiantly to take control of herself. As I watched her coping with her tears, hugging the mauled copy of *The Little Prince* to her chest and relentlessly plaguing me with questions about what was happening and why, I knew she would make it. She was strong; probably stronger than I. My work with the emotionally disturbed had deeply impressed upon me their resilience. Despite many popular notions, they were far from fragile. To have survived at all was testimony of this. Given the tools that so many of us take for granted, given love and support and trust and self-value that we often do not notice when we have it, they go beyond survival to prevail. In Sheila this was self-evident. She would not give up trying.

In the midst of all the flurry over the ending of the school year, my birthday came. We made a big thing about birthdays in our room, partly because most of the children did not get a celebration anywhere else and partly because I like parties. It seemed only reasonable that the kids should get to celebrate Anton's and Whitney's and my birthdays as well. After all, we had all been born too, and I did not have the modesty to pretend it did not matter. So when my birthday came I brought in a big yellow elephant-shaped cake and chocolate ice cream.

The day did not go well. Nothing especially terrible happened, just the little annoying things that kids seem to be best at doing. Peter had gotten in a fight on the bus and arrived with a bloody nose and a grudge. During recess Sarah got mad at Sheila, who in turn got mad at Tyler, who cried. Then Sheila kicked sand on Sarah and she cried. The quiet corner did a booming business all day long. However, it wasn't until afternoon that I lost my patience. When Whitney went down to the teachers' lounge for the ice cream, she found out one of the fifth grade classes had mistakenly thought it was theirs. I set the cake out anyway. Peter and William were horsing around with each other while we were getting ready. They had a couple of blocks which they were pretending to juggle. I had asked them to stop but they hadn't. One of the other kids was pulling on my arm and I was momentarily distracted. Then *crash*. William had thrown a block to Peter who, while backing up to catch it, bumped into Sheila sitting on the floor. He fell on her and they both came up swinging. Before I knew it Sheila had one of the blocks poised to throw at Peter. He picked up a chair and flung it angrily in her direction. The chair hit the table, then Max, then the cake. My yellow elephant splattered.

"Okay, you guys, that *is* it!" I shouted. "Every single one of you in your chairs with your heads down."

"But it wasn't my fault," Guillermo protested. "I didn't do anything.'"

"Everybody."

All the kids, even Max and Freddie, found chairs and sat down. Everyone except Sheila.

"It don't be my fault dumb old Peter tripped on me." She was sitting on the floor where Peter had knocked her.

"Get in a chair and put your head down like everybody else. I've had it with the whole lot of you. All you've done all day is bicker. Well, this is where it gets you. Sitting in a chair with your head down."

Sheila remained on the floor.

"Sheila, get up."

With a great sigh she rose and took a chair. Pulling it over next to Tyler, she sat and put her head down.

I looked at them. What a ragtag lot. Whitney and Anton were picking cake out of the carpet. Anton rolled his eyes when I came over. I smiled wearily. What I really felt like doing was crying. For no particular reason except that I had wanted a special day and had gotten an ordinary one. And for my yellow elephant cake that had taken so much time to make and ended up being ground into the rug.

When I turned around to look at the kids, Peter had one eye peering over the side of his arm. I pointed a finger at him and gave him the evil eye. He covered his face again. I looked at the clock and watched the second hand revolve.

"Okay, you guys, if you can act like human beings you can get up. There's about ten minutes left. Help pick up the rest of the cake and then find something quiet to do I better not hear one single word of fighting."

Sheila remained at the table with her head down.

"Sheil, you can get up."

She remained unmoving, her head in her arms. I came over to her and sat down in a chair beside her. "I'm not so mad anymore. You can get up and play."

"Uh-uh," she said. "This here's my birthday present for you. I ain't gonna be no trouble for the rest of the day."

After school Whitney took Sheila out and Anton and I went down to the teachers' lounge. I was sitting in the one comfortable chair, my head back, my feet up on the table, my arm over my eyes.

"What a hell of a day," I said. When Anton did not respond I sat up and opened my eyes. He was gone. I had not even heard him leave. Oh, well, I leaned back again. I almost fell asleep.

"Tor?"

I looked up. Anton was back, standing over my chair.

"Happy Birthday." He handed me a fat envelope.

"Hey, you shouldn't have done anything. That's the deal around here."

He grinned. "Open it."

Inside was a crazy cartoon card with a green snake on it. Out fell a piece of folded paper.

"What's this?" I asked.

"My present to you."

I opened the paper. It was the photostated copy of a letter.

Dear Mr. Antonio Ramirez:
  With great pleasure Cherokee County Community College announces that you have been chosen as one of the recipients of the Dalton E. Fellows Scholarship.
  Congratulations. We look forward to seeing you in our program this fall.

I looked up at him. Even though he was trying, he could not keep the smile on his lips in check. It spread from ear to ear. I wanted to congratulate him. To tell him how much this piece of paper pleased me. I said nothing. We just stared at each other. And smiled.

I had called Ed about Sheila's future placement and we held a team meeting. I continued to hold out for placing Sheila with my friend, Sandy McGuire, at Jefferson Elementary School. Sandy was a young, sensitive teacher whom I could trust not to lose Sheila in the crowd. She had talked to me about Sheila a number of times when I had first had the notion that Sheila might be ready to go back to a normal setting.

At first Ed did not favor the plan. He disliked advancing children ahead of their chronological peer group. Moreover, Sheila was a small child for her age. Most of the eight- and nine-year-olds would be half a head above her. We did a lot of soul-searching. She was at least two grades ahead of the second graders academically and she was smaller than they were as well. In her case there were no perfect solutions. I was more in favor of placing her with a teacher I could trust to continue supporting her emotional growth than worrying about her size or IQ. Clearly, she would never be normal academically, so there was no point in providing a source of new trouble. I feared that Sheila's unchained mind would go so unchallenged in second grade that she would get into trouble just keeping herself occupied. In the end the team agreed to try Sheila in Sandy's room. She would also get two hours a day in a resource room to help meet her emotional needs and her advanced academic status.

The second to the last week of school I told Sheila she would be at Jefferson the following year. I said I knew her teacher very well and that we had been friends a long time. I asked Sheila if she would like to go visit Sandy in her classroom some day after school. The first time I suggested it was coupled with telling her where she was going the next year. Sheila could not accept that all at once and vehemently announced that she would not now nor would she ever want to meet Sandy. But later in the day, after the other kids had heard of Sheila's placement and had been all excited because she was skipping a grade, Sheila decided that she might not mind meeting Sandy so much after all.

Wednesday afternoon Sheila and I climbed into my little car right after the bell rang and started off for Jefferson Elementary on the other side of town. Because we had almost a half hour before Sandy's class was finished at three thirty, I stopped at Baskin-Robbins for ice cream cones. Sheila selected a double scoop of licorice. The mistake I made was in not taking any napkins with us when we got back into the car.

By the time we arrived at Jefferson, Sheila looked as if she had changed races. She had black ice cream all over her cheeks and chin, on her hair and down the front of her shirt. I looked at her in surprise because only fifteen minutes earlier she had been clean. I did not even have a Kleenex with me, so I wiped what I could off with my hand. With Sheila clutching at me tightly we went to see the school.

Sandy laughed when she saw Sheila. I couldn't blame her. Sheila looked like a four-year-old with all that ice cream on her and her fear gave her a waif-like solemnity. She pressed close to my leg.

"Boy, you look like you had something good," Sandy said, smiling. "What was it?"

Sheila stared at her wide-eyed. "Ice cream," she whispered. I wondered what Sandy must have been thinking just then. I had enticed her into accepting Sheila mostly by elaborating on Sheila's incredible giftedness and verbal ability. Right then Sheila sounded anything but the epitome of intelligence.

212

I should have trusted Sandy more. Bringing over chairs, she sat down with us and proceeded to get all the details of Sheila's ice cream passions. Then she took us on a tour of the room. It was a typical-looking classroom. Jefferson was an ancient, bulky, brick building with huge rooms. The room easily accommodated twenty-seven desks and a variety of "learning centers" around the perimeter. As usual for Sandy's room, it was messy. Stacks of workbooks defied gravity on the corner of a table, bits of construction paper were strewn through the aisles. I had never been known for my neatness, but Sandy's clutter surpassed even mine. The children must have had half-a-dozen projects going in all states of completion. In the back of the room was a well-stocked bookcase and a gerbil cage.

Slowly Sheila began to thaw out and come to life. The books interested her and finally got the better of her timidity. Soon she was wandering around on her own, inspecting the premises. Sandy flashed me a toothy, knowing smile as we watched Sheila in silence. She'd make it.

Standing on tiptoe to see the covers of the workbooks, Sheila took one from the top of the stack and paged through it. Still holding it, she came over to me. "This here's different than them you got, Torey," she said.

"That's probably the kind you'd use in here."

She continued to look through it. Then she turned to Sandy. "I don't like doing workbooks so well."

Sandy pursed her lips and nodded slowly. "I've heard other kids say that too. They aren't a lot of fun, are they?"

Sheila eyed her a moment. "I do 'em though. Torey makes me. I didn't used to, but I do now. This here one don't look too bad. I'd probably do this one." She examined a page carefully. "This here kid made a mistake. Look, it gots a red mark by it." She showed it to me.

"Sometimes people make mistakes," Sandy said. I made a mental note to tell her of Sheila's allergy to correction. That would be one of next year's tasks: reducing Sheila's anxiety about her errors.

"What d'you do to them?" Sheila asked.

"When they make a mistake?" Sandy said. "Oh, I just ask them to do it over again. If they don't understand, I help them. Everybody goofs up once in a while. It's no big deal."

"Do you whip kids?"

With a grin Sandy shook her head. "Nope. I sure don't."

Sheila nodded toward me. "Torey, she don't either."

We stayed with Sandy for almost forty-five minutes, Sheila becoming bolder and bolder with her questions. Finally, I suggested we leave so we would get back in time for Sheila's bus. As we went out the door, Sandy mentioned that perhaps Sheila would like to come over for part of a day before school let out and see how it was in the third grade when the children were there. I thanked her for her time and we trotted out to the car.

Sheila was quiet through most of the ride back to our school. Just as I turned the car into the parking lot, Sheila turned to me. "She ain't so bad, I guess."

"Good, I'm glad you liked her."

We climbed out of the car. Sheila took my hand as we walked toward the building. "Tor, do you suppose I could go over to Miss McGuire's class sometime?"

"You want to?"

"I wouldn't really mind."

I nodded. Stretching up to pick a dogwood flower off the tree that leaned over the school doorway, I fastened it into her hair. "Yeah, Sheil, I reckon we could arrange that for you."

Monday of the final week Anton drove Sheila over to Sandy's class. She had elected to remain the entire day, although I had suggested she go just for the morning. But she wanted to eat in the cafeteria, paying for her own lunch and getting to select what she wanted to eat like the other children. At our school my class was the last to eat and their trays were all fixed for them and laid out on the table. Sheila wanted to see how it felt to be a regular kid. My heart lurched a little watching her leave with Anton, her small hand in his. She had come wearing the red, white and blue dress Chad had bought her rather than her everyday jeans and shirt that we had gotten with the money her father had given me. She asked me to put her hair in a ponytail and had found a piece of yarn from the scrap box to tie around

t. She looked so tiny next to Anton as they left, and so vulnerable.

Sheila returned that afternoon a satisfied veteran. The day had gone smoothly and she smiled with pride as she related how she had carried her own lunch tray clear across the cafeteria without spilling anything, and how a girl named Maria, who had the longest, shiniest, prettiest black hair she'd ever seen, had saved a place for Sheila to eat with her. There had been hitches. She had lost her way coming back from the girls' restroom. In the tone of voice she used telling the incident, I gathered she must have been very frightened to find herself in such a spot. But she finally made it back. And, she smiled proudly, she never let on to anybody that she'd been lost. At recess she discovered the long dress, despite its being so pretty, was an impediment to play. She tripped while running and skinned her knees. Sheila pulled the dress up to show me. The scratches weren't very visible, but they hurt, she informed me. She hadn't cried about it. Sandy had seen it happen and had given Sheila comfort. Beaming, Sheila told me Sandy smelled good when she held you real close and she would blow on your knees 'til they felt better. All in all, it had been a successful day. Sheila affirmed that it would be an okay class to be in although she hoped Maria flunked, so she'd still be in it next year and they could be friends. I hastened to mention Maria and she might still be friends without wishing poor Maria such bad luck. For the first time Sheila did not get that stricken look about leaving my class; she didn't even mention it. Instead, her conversation was punctuated with "Next year, Miss McGuire says I can . . ." or "Miss McGuire's going to let me . . . when I'm in her room next year." It was a sweet-sad moment for me because I knew I had been outgrown.

On the last day of school we had a picnic. I contacted everybody's parents and a number met us over in the park a few blocks from school. We brought packed lunches from the cafeteria and the makings for ice cream sundaes, while the parents brought cookies and other goodies. The park was a huge one, old and sprawling with a small zoo and a large duck pond. It had gardens of flowers all gleaming in the June sunshine. Children scattered in every direction with a parent in tow.

Sheila's father did not come; we had not really expected him. But when Sheila showed up in the morning she was dressed in a bright orange-and-white sunsuit. She seemed embarrassed about having so much of herself exposed and walked around clutching her body for the first half hour with us. But Anton raved about the beautiful color and teased her about stealing it if he got the chance. This loosened her up in a fit of giggles at the thought of Anton wearing her sunsuit and she danced for us across the floor of the classroom while we waited for the other children. Her father had bought the sunsuit for her the night before at the discount store and it was the first new thing she could ever remember him getting her. Her mirth bubbled up in her so brightly that she could not stay still. All the way to the park she pirouetted down the sidewalk, her blond hair swirling in the air as she turned.

Once at the park she continued her joyous movements and Anton and Whitney and I sat in the sun by the duck pond after lunch and watched her. She was apart from us, thirty or forty feet down the walk that circled the pond. She was listening to some inner music and gliding in harmony around on the sidewalk. Others on the walk had to step around her, their faces amused. A skip, now a twirl, then a few rhythmic bends. It was almost eerie watching her dance alone in the sunlight, her hair glistening in a wide yellow wheel. Completely oblivious to the strollers on the walk, to the other children, to Anton and Whitney and me, she satisfied some inner dream to dance. The others must have felt the same eldritch fascination that I did. Anton watched without speaking. Whitney cocked her head as if trying to catch the music none of us was hearing.

Anton turned to me. "She looks like a spirit, doesn't she? Like if you blinked too hard, she'd be gone."

I nodded.

"She's free," Whitney said softly. And that indeed was what she was.

The end of the day came all too quickly. We packed up our things and returned to the classroom to pass out the last of the papers and say our final good-byes. The narrow, wood-paneled room was almost empty now. Pictures and stories were down from the walls. The animals had all gone to my apartment. The names were removed from the cubbies.

The finality of what was happening dawned on Sheila and she lost her merry spirit. By the time we had given out all the papers and awaited the ringing of the bell to go home, Sheila had retreated to the corner, empty now of its pillows and animal cages. Lacking those, she squatted on the floor. The other children were all chattering, excited about summer vacation and their changes for next year. So while Anton led them in songs, I broke away to Sheila.

The tears coursed silently over her now-tanned cheeks. Without a Kleenex, she used her hair to wipe away the wetness. Her eyes were filled with hurt and sorrow. "I don't wanna go," she wailed. "I don't want this to be over. I wanna come back, Torey."

"Of course you do, honey." I took her in my arms. "But that's just how it feels now. In just a little while you'll have a whole summer ahead of you and then you'll be in third grade, a regular kid. It's just a little hard right now, that's all."

"I don't wanna go, Torey. And I don't want you to go."

I smoothed away her bangs. "Remember, I told you I'd write you letters. We'll still know what's happening to each other. It won't be like we're really apart. You'll see."

"No, I won't. I want to stay." She was struggling to regain control and her wiry little body shuddered in my arms. "I'm gonna be bad. I'm not gonna be nice at all in Miss McGuire's class and then you'll have to come back."

"Hey, I don't want to hear that. That's the old Sheila talking."

"I won't be good. I won't. And you can't make me."

"No, Sheil, I can't. That's your decision. But you know it won't change things any. It won't make this year come back or this class. Or me. I'll be going to school myself, like I told you. What you do with yourself only you can decide. But it won't bring this year back."

She was staring at the floor, her bottom lip pushed out.

I smiled. "Remember, you tamed me. You're responsible for me. That means we'll never forget we love each other. That means we'll probably cry a little right now. But pretty soon we'll only remember how happy we were with each other."

She shook her head. "I won't ever be happy."

Just then the bell rang and the room was alive with shouts. I rose and went to the other children. Hesitantly Sheila trailed over too. The good-byes came. Tyler and William were teary-eyed. Peter whooped with joy. We all exchanged hugs and kisses and they were gone, running out into the June warmth.

Sheila was catching the high school bus back to the migrant camp. On this last day, it left only a short time after the bus for the grade school children. I figured that, after saying good-bye to Anton and Whitney and collecting her things, Sheila would have just enough time to walk the two blocks to the high school and meet her bus.

Parting from Anton was hard for her. At first she covered her face and refused to even look at him. He kept coaxing her to smile, saying little things in Spanish, which I did not understand but Sheila did. After all, he reminded her, they'd still see each other at the migrant camp. He promised to bring her over to play with his two little boys. Finally I delivered an ultimatum. I'd walk her to her bus, but she had to leave right away. With this she turned to Anton and hugged him, her tiny arms locking him in a wrestler's hold. Then she waved to Whitney and took my hand. At the doorway she paused, broke away and ran to hug Anton again. She kissed his cheek and trotted back to me. Tears sparkled as she picked up her things, a few papers and the worn copy of *The Little Prince*, a tangible memory of what had been. We descended the steps and went down the walk to the high school.

She did not speak the entire way. Neither did I. We had gone beyond needing words. Talking would have spoiled what we had. The bus was waiting in the semicircle drive of the high school, but the students had not yet loaded. The bus driver waved to us and Sheila ran over to put her things on a seat. The she came out of the bus again, walking back to where I stood.

She looked up at me, shading her eyes from the light. I looked at her. It seemed a small eternity in the bright sunlight. "Bye," she said very softly.

I sank to my knees and embraced her. My heart was roaring in my ears, my throat too tight to speak. Then I rose and she ran to the bus. All the way to the steps of the bus she ran, but as she started up them she stopped. The older kids were there now and she had to wait to get in. She looked over at me. Then suddenly she came running back.

"I didn't mean it," she said breathlessly. "I didn't mean it when I said I would be bad. I'll be a good girl." She looked up solemnly. "For you."

I shook my head. "No, not for me. You be good for you."

She smiled slightly, oddly. Then in a second she was gone, back to the bus already, scurrying up the stairs and disappearing. In moments I saw her face at the rear window, pressed tight against the glass. The driver shut the door and the bus began to rumble. "Bye," she was mouthing, her nose squashed flat against the window. I could not tell if she was crying. The bus pulled around and down the drive. A small hand waved, frantically at first then more gently. I raised my hand and smiled as the bus turned onto the street and disappeared from sight.

"Bye-bye," I said, the words squeezing themselves almost inaudibly from my stricken throat. Then I turned to go back.

Epilogue

In the mail a year ago came a crumpled, water-stained piece of notebook paper inscribed in blue felt-tip marker. No letter accompanied it.

To Torey with much
"Love"

All the rest came
They tried to make me laugh
They played their games with me
Some games for fun and some for keeps
And then they went away
Leaving me in the ruins of games
Not knowing which were for keeps and
Which were for fun and
Leaving me alone with the echoes of
Laughter that was not mine.

Then you came
With your funny way of being

Not quite human
And you made me cry
And you didn't seem to care if I did
You just said the games are over
And waited
Until all my tears turned into
Joy.

MARY

by Patricia Collins

A CHILD YOU'LL WANT TO REMEMBER.

Mary Collins was a really beautiful baby. Born prematurely, she had a tiny oval face, a rosebud mouth and an enchanting smile. The third child of parents who came from the bustle of New York to make a home in Ireland, Mary found a warm and secure place in the heart of the family.

Then, eight months later, Patricia Collins learned that Mary was brain damaged. Doctors diagnosed cerebral palsy; she would probably never walk and she would almost certainly be retarded.

The shock of this discovery plunged Patricia into despair. Mary needed extensive therapy and the burden of caring for her increased Patricia's growing resentment and guilt – she began to drink heavily, blaming herself for what had happened. When circumstances forced the Collins family to return to America, Patricia made a wrenching decision to leave Mary behind in Ireland in a residential home for two years. The years in Ireland did nothing to lessen the severity of Mary's disabilities, but another kind of change did occur. Mary was becoming a determined, courageous child with a winning personality and she gave a very special purpose and meaning to life.

This is an intimate, inspiring and deeply moving account of a mother's journey from despair to joy and of the power of the human spirit to overcome adversity through love and understanding.

A STORY YOU WON'T FORGET.

BIOGRAPHY   0 7221 2482 1   £1.5

THE HEARTWARMING TRUE STORY
OF A VERY SPECIAL DOG
AND HER VERY SPECIAL OWNER

SHEILA HOCKEN

EMMA V.I.P.

(Illus)

veryone knows the inspiring story of Sheila Hocken and
er wonderful guide-dog Emma, and of the miracle
peration which enabled her to see for the first time in her
fe.

ow, Sheila describes her life since the incredible moment
hen she opened her eyes and saw the beautiful world we
l take for granted. With freshness and humour, Sheila
lls how each day brought new joys, new challenges and
ew surprises.

mma's life, too, has undergone dramatic changes. She was
o longer needed as a guide-dog but her retirement has
een far from idle. She is now a celebrity and receives her
wn fan mail; she has made several television appearances;
he was Personality Dog of the Year at Crufts and is greeted
the street more often than Sheila is.

Writing simply, with innate ability to externalise thought,
eeling, experience, she again achieves a lovable intimacy'
aily Telegraph

AUTOBIOGRAPHY   0 7221 4601 9   £1.25

Also by Sheila Hocken in Sphere Books:
EMMA AND I

A selection of bestsellers from SPHERE

FICTION

REMEMBRANCE	Danielle Steel	£1.95
BY THE GREEN OF THE SPRING	John Masters	£2.50
MISSION	Patrick Tilley	£1.95
DECEPTIONS	Judith Michael	£3.95
THREE WOMEN	Nancy Thayer	£1.75

FILM & TV TIE-INS

E.T. THE EXTRA-TERRESTRIAL	William Kotzwinkle	£1.50
FAME	Leonore Fleischer	£1.50
CONAN THE BARBARIAN	L. Sprague de Camp & Lin Carter	£1.25
THE SWORD AND THE SORCERER	Norman Winski	£1.50
GREASE 2	William Rotsler	£1.25

NON-FICTION

ONE CHILD	Torey L. Hayden	£1.75
DAM-BURST OF DREAMS	Christopher Nolan	£1.75
THE COUNTRYSIDE COOKBOOK	Gail Duff	£5.95
GREAT RAILWAY JOURNEYS OF THE WORLD		£5.95

All Sphere books are available at your local bookshop or newsagent, or can be ordered direct from the publisher. Just tick the titles you want and fill in the form below.

Name _____

Address _____

_____

Write to Sphere Books, Cash Sales Department, P.O. Box 11, Falmouth, Cornwall TR10 9EN

Please enclose a cheque or postal order to the value of the cover price plus:

UK: 45p for the first book, 20p for the second book and 14p per copy for each additional book ordered to a maximum charge of £1.63.

OVERSEAS: 75p for the first book and 21p for each additional book.

BFPO & EIRE: 45p for the first book, 20p for the second book plus 14p per copy for the next 7 books, thereafter 8p per book.

Sphere Books reserve the right to show new retail prices on covers which may differ from those previously advertised in the text or elsewhere and to increase postal rates in accordance with the PO.